DISCOVER & AWAKE THE Champion IN YOU

ACHIEVING YOUR PURPOSE IN LIFE

GIDEON O. OJO

DISCOVER & AWAKE THE CHAMPION IN YOU
Copyright © 2019
Gideon Oyedele Ojo
Watob Impact Publisher
www.watobimpact.com
watobimpact@yahoo.com

Unless otherwise stated all Scripture quotations are taken from the New International Version of the Holy Bible.

ISBN: 9781087812366

ALL RIGHTS RESERVED.

No part of this book may be reproduced in any form without permission of the Author except for brief quotations and critical reviews.

For further enquiries or information please contact:
Watob Impact LLC:
watobimpact@yahoo.com

Published in the USA

TABLE OF CONTENT

Chapter 1 - The Champion	21-39
Chapter 2 - Road Map to Championship	43-51
Chapter 3 - Pathways to Championship	57-65
Chapter 4 - Attributes of A Champion	71-77
Chapter 5 - Requirements of Championship	83-92
Chapter 6 - The Test of a Champion	97-104
Chapter 7 - The Champion in You	109-116
Chapter 8 - Turning your Potential to Reality	121-134
Chapter 9 - The Core of Every Champion	139-144
Chapter 10 - A-Z Character Traits of a Champion	149-152
Chapter 11 - Jesus Christ the Greatest Champion	157-164
Conclusion	169-175
References	176

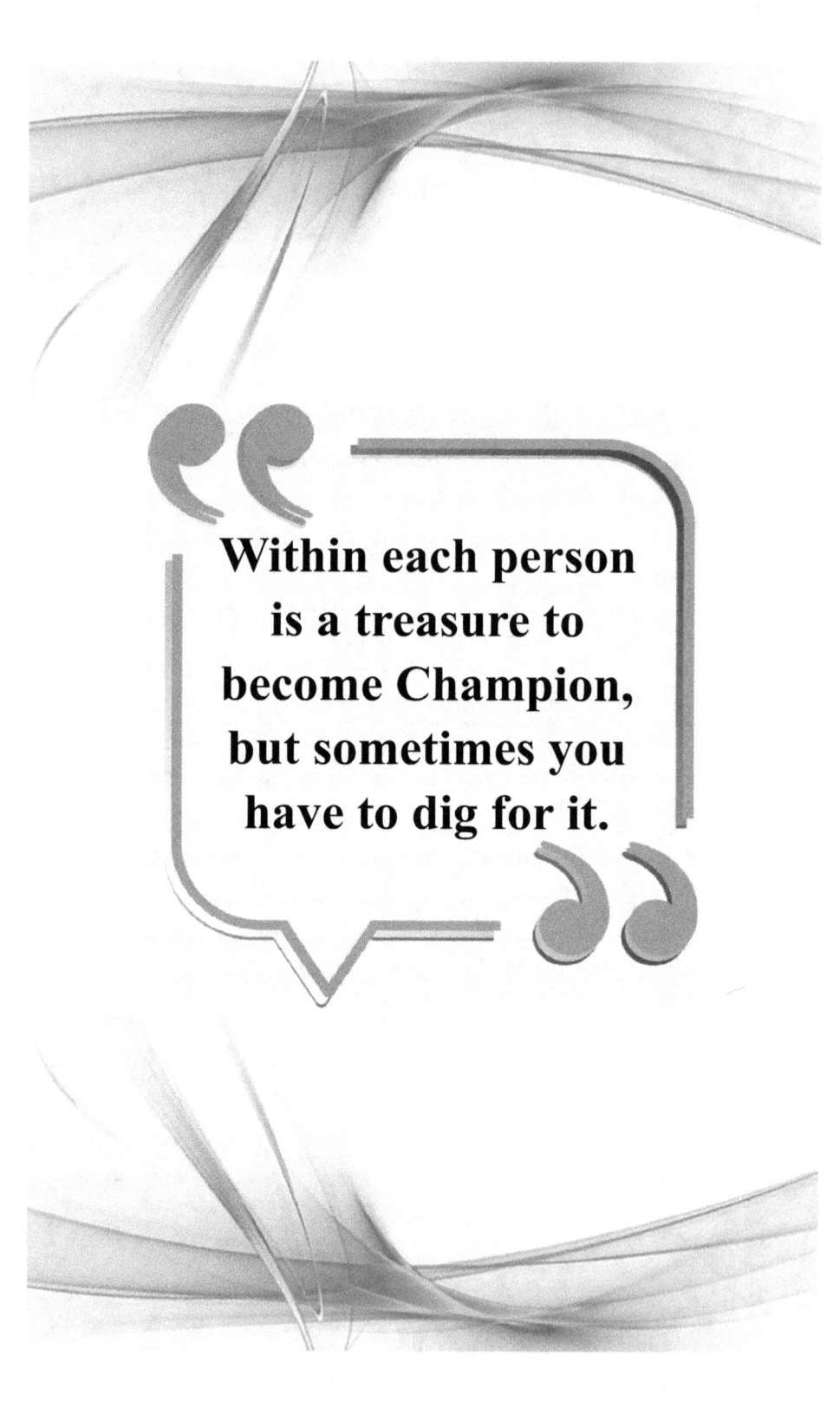

> Within each person is a treasure to become Champion, but sometimes you have to dig for it.

Acknowledgements

One of the scriptures that I find profoundly encouraging all the time is by Apostle Paul in Philippians 4:13 – "I can do ALL THINGS through Christ who strengthens me."

Having said this, I will like to thank the Almighty God, who inspired and strengthened me to complete this book. My God and my Father, without you, I can do nothing. I appreciate you Lord for planting this book in my mind, with your spirit working in my heart and gently bringing it to fruition. I return all glory and honor unto you because you are my wisdom, knowledge, and understanding.

To my Pastors- Nathaniel & Jumoke Saingbe, here is the fruit of your prayers, teachings, and encouragement. I sincerely appreciate the integrity of your lives, the anointing upon you, and your dedication to God's kingdom.

To Mrs. Ronke Adesina and Olawale Abaire, I owe much of the credit for this book, for their writing assistance, constructive feedback, proofreading, and editing skills.

I will like to express my immense appreciation to Chikezie Gloria Iniobong, my personal assistant, both at home and abroad. Thanks for designing the cover page, formatting the inside pages and all the other assistants that I cannot recount. God bless you and your families.

To my brothers: Mr. Ranti Lajide, Bisola Ojo and Larry Ojo who encouraged and assisted me at various stages. I say thank you.

To all those, whose names I have not mentioned, but contributed to this book at one time or the other, I say thank you.

To my faithful wife, Abiola, who kept me going all the time, thank you for your encouragement and support to pursue my dream with dogged determination. Your sacrifice of love, hard work, and patience are treasured gifts to me. We have come a long way, but I will never forget where we began.

To my children – The WATOB, the Lord keep you. I am proud of you and what God has been doing in your lives. I appreciate the love and support we receive from you all the time.

DEDICATION

Now to Him who is able to do exceedingly abundantly above all that we ask or think, according to the power that works in us, to Him be glory in the church by Christ Jesus to all generations, forever and ever, amen. – Ephesians 3:20-21, and

To my wife & children, who made the Journey along with me, this book is fondly dedicated.

PREFACE

My purpose for writing this book is to help you unveil and discover the purpose for which God created you into this world; to encourage you to strive more to be what God wants you to be and to stir up the giant in you to be a Champion. No doubt, there is a seed God planted in you when you were being created; the seeds are potentials for everyone to succeed in life and to bring glory to God. You cannot afford to be a waste because you are valuable to God. You are God's offspring created in His image, full of potentials, raw talents, and abilities, not only to succeed as Champion but to also to help others and to glorify God.

> **"For we are God's handiwork, created in Christ Jesus to do good works, which God prepared in advance for us to do."**
> *-Ephesians 2:10 (NIV)*

There is something in you that is not in another person created by the same God. Even identical twins who share the same womb are endowed differently, as Champions, by God for different assignments here on earth. You are unique and distinctly created with potentials that give you the ability to become the Champion God had in mind. You are purposely created to carry out an assignment.

> "I will praise thee, for I am wonderfully made; marvelous are thy works…"
> -Psalm 139:14 (KJV)

You are a Champion material any day, any time.
You are not here by accident. Your birth is not a mistake, because God doesn't make or do anything by accident. God has a reason for everything he creates. He has a reason and purpose for creating you. Your life has a profound meaning because there is a God who made you for a reason; a purpose, and you have something to offer to humanity that is unique. God's ultimate desire is for you to be a Champion in this life and also in eternity. You are of great worth to God. God knows you and knows what he wants you to be before creating you.

> "For I know the plans I have for you," declares the Lord, "plans to prosper you and not to harm you, plans to give you hope and a future."
> -Jer. 29:11 (NIV)

God is your maker, your creator, the author, and finisher of your faith. He knows you inside out even ahead of your being created. No wonder the Psalmist says,

> "My frame was not hidden from you when I was made secret place....You saw me before I was born. Every day my life was recorded in your book. Every moment was laid out before a single day had passed".
> *-Psalm 139:15-16*

The plan of God for you is not ambiguous but very clear. His plan is for you to prosper, to succeed, and to be a Champion. You are God's unique offspring full of potentials to be a Champion in every area of life. The potentials are lying dormant in you, not yet tapped and yet to be used. The seeds in you need to die and germinate to produce a tree that will bear fruits.

> "Verily, verily, I say unto you, Except a corn of wheat falls into the ground and dies, it abideth alone: but if it dies, it bringeth forth much fruit."
> *- John 12:24 (KJV)*

You need to allow God's seed in your life to germinate. God is in charge of your life, but your destiny is in your hands as he has planned it. Nothing could stop you from becoming the Champion that God has destined you to be.

God created you so that you could bring glory to Him, and you can only bring glory to Him by fulfilling the purpose for which you have been created.

> "For of him, and through him, and to him, are all things: to whom be glory forever."
> *-Romans 11:36 (KJV)*

Whatever the situation you may be in now, you can still turn things around. It is time to take back your life and be focused as the Champion that God has proposed for you to be. Whatever you have gone through before now is just a stepping stone to your greatness. You can do it! It does not matter your past failures, your bad experiences, your past mistakes, and your situation now. God knows everything about you, and he wants to help you.

> **"The Lord will fulfill his purpose for me."**
> *-Psalm 38:8a*

You have got to trust God to fulfill his purpose in your life. No one can reach his potential in life without the father's help. God who created you created you uniquely. He made you one of a kind. He knows your beginning and has your end in his palm. Every experience of life you have before now are simply essential learning experiences for you to be a Champion. It is time for you to focus on God, hold your destiny, and fulfill your purpose. You have got to pick up your mat and walk. Forget about excuses and stories, break out, get loose, just like the story of the man who has been invalid for thirty-eight years at the pool of Bethesda (John 5:1-8). I prophesy into your life that everything that has tied you down before now will get loose for you to fulfill your purpose. Start living a rewarding life, a fulfilled life, a life of Champion in the name that is above any other name, in Jesus name. Enlarge your vision, be the best God wants you to be- a Champion.

INTRODUCTION

Your future begins with what is in your hand today

I once heard the story of a man who was described to be undefeated in his camp, among his people, and in his nation; a champion so-called. However, on a particular day, during a great battle between his nation and another, over territorial influence, the battle was drawn, and the condition of the battle was defined to be a fight among champions from the two nations. The nation of the Champion that loses would have to serve the other nation. This particular Champion, dressed in his war regalia was a man of full stature and terrorizing look. He was full of rage and kept screaming at the other nation to bring forth their so-called Champion, but for days, the terrorized nation could not provide a champion to face this proclaimed Champion. Days went by and daily, they awoke to hear the terrorizing Champion calling out to them to defend their nation from slavery, but the story reported that this champion-less country lived in great fear all through those days.

It won't be unnatural to wonder if no man could be found to defend this great but terrified nation before the mighty and raging Champion. This book unfolds the answer to the puzzle. To fully understand the subject of this book, we need to premise our discussions on some background knowledge: where you are coming from, where you are and where you are heading to.

> **Learn from yesterday, live for today, hope for tomorrow- Albert Einstein**

Life can be described as a dash between two dates, birth and death. That is why two dates, with a dash in between them, are placed in obituaries. To be a champion, there is great wisdom in recognizing the wisdom of the time. Life is a matter of time, which, once spent, can never be regained. God is so kind in his infinite mercy that He gives every man 24 hours a day with no bias, sentiment, or discrimination. How you use your own 24 hours towards becoming the champion that God has destined you to be depend on you. It is the part of your time that was already spent that has produced who you are today. Your yesterday, your today and your tomorrow are parts of a continuum called your life. All the three are essential and must be handled cautiously to achieve success as champions. No wonder the word of God says:

> **"So teach us to number our days, That we may gain a heart of wisdom."** *Psalms 90:12*

YESTERDAY:
Your yesterday is the part of your life that had already been spent. It is the

period of your birth and the last one second. Your yesterday is not retrievable as it has become part of your life history. You can only look back at it but can never go back to it. Life must definitely continue. No matter how much you wish it, you cannot revert back to your yesterday. Do not let what happened yesterday inhibit your today or tomorrow. The only valuable thing in your yesterday is the lesson you can learn from it that can make you a champion. Extract these lessons and turn them to useful data for the calculation of today's motion and tomorrow's championship. Once you have extracted the lessons from yesterday, bury it and let it rest in perfect peace.

TODAY:

Today is now, yesterday is gone. Nothing can be done about your yesterday and your tomorrow, but a lot can be done today. Your today is cumulative of all your yesterday experiences. Your yesterday has made what you are today. Your now is the product of your then. On his way out, your yesterday has deposited some things into your life that has made you what you are today. Your yesterday has gone, and not much can be achieved from it any longer. Your concentration now is on your today. Worry about today before tomorrow. If you want to be a champion, then, you must be careful to handle today properly; handled it with care so that it will not distort your today or jeopardize your tomorrow. The best preparation to become tomorrow's champion is doing your best today. Do not postpone what you need to do today that will make your tomorrow. What you do or not do determine your tomorrow. Spend your today wisely. Start from where you are today, all the great men you hear about started from somewhere. Live for the present plan for the future.

TOMORROW:

Tomorrow is the day after today. A day you have never seen or witnessed before. It is on its way. It is the future, and it is dependent on how you handle today. To become a champion, you must integrate and synthesize your yesterday, consolidate, with passion, on your today, and strive with a tenacity to achieve a successful tomorrow. You need to be more positive, strategic, and push harder today than you did yesterday to have a breakthrough tomorrow. You cannot wait until tomorrow, tomorrow starts now!

BREAK FROM YESTERDAY:

When a man refuses to part with what was gone, he loses the focus of what is coming. Thank God for your past. Everyone has a past, which is a blend of the good, the bad, and the ugly. No matter what it was,, your past is gone. You cannot continue to dwell on your yesterday. As long as you keep to brood over the odds of yesterday, you will not be able to rise up to the victory ahead that will turn you to a champion. If you think about the past too much, you may not enjoy the present. Paul says;

> "Brothers and sisters, I do not consider myself yet to have taken hold of it. But one thing I do: Forgetting what is behind and straining toward what is ahead. I press on toward the goals to win the prize for which God has called me heavenward in Christ Jesus".
> -*Philippians 3:13-14*

Break yourself from yesterday and face the reality of today to achieve tomorrow's success. Free yourself from yesterday's burdens, so as not to add to today's weight. The more you concentrate your efforts on the past, the less of what is ahead you can see.

"The past can chain you up, but the future can set you free"

> "Forget the former things; do not dwell on the past."
> -Isaiah 43:18

However, the fact that you must not be burdened with a load of yesterday does not suggest that you should live as if you have no past. Your yesterday should be your history to teach you lessons on how to handle today and tomorrow. If you don't learn from your yesterday, you may make the same mistakes of yesterday.

> "Now all these things happened to them as examples, and they were written for our admonition, upon whom the ends of the ages have come."
> -1 Corinthians 10:11

The only valuable thing in your yesterday is the lessons you can learn from it. Once you pick the lessons, bury it and move forward.

> "See, I am doing a new thing! Now it springs up; do you not perceive it? I am making a way in the wilderness and streams in the wasteland".
> Isaiah 43:19

God is setting a new way before you. Can you see it? There is something you can do that will take you to the platform of champions, where God has destined you to be. Come out of the past, take a new step, and be courageous, as you take a step of faith to do what God has inspired you to do in life. Be a champion.

Oprah Winfrey

Oprah Winfrey was born in 1954 at Kosciusko, Mississippi. Her early life was not without thorns; her parents were unmarried and separated soon after conception, leaving Oprah with a difficult childhood. She lived in great poverty and often had to dress in potato sacks for which she was mocked at school. She was also sexually abused at an early age. From the age of 14, she went to live with her father. Oprah says he was strict, but she was in the mood to be disobedient during her teenage years. After working her way through college, she became interested in journalism and media and got her first job as a news anchor for a local TV station.

Her emotional style did not go down well for a news program, so she was transferred to an ailing daytime chat program. After Oprah had taken over, the daily chat show took off, and this later led to her own program– The Oprah Winfrey Show.

Oprah Winfrey, influential talk show host, author, philanthropist, actress, and media personality has played a vital role in modern American life, shaping cultural trends and promoting various liberal causes. Through her talk shows and books, she has focused on many issues facing American women. She has been a famous role model for black American women, breaking down many invisible barriers. Oprah has also remained a powerful role model for women and black American women in particular. She is credited with promoting an intimate confessional form of media communication, which has been imitated across the globe.

Some of her famous quotes include:

"Turn your wounds into wisdom."

(https://www.brainyquote.com/quotes/oprah_winfrey_103803)

"What I learned at a very early age was that I was responsible for my life. And as I became more spiritually conscious, I learned that we all are responsible for ourselves, that you create your own reality by the way you think and therefore act. You cannot blame apartheid, your parents, your circumstances, because you are not your circumstances. You are your possibilities. If you know that, you can do anything."

(https://www.brainyquote.com/quotes/oprah_winfrey_383916).

Her range of media enterprises has made Oprah one of the richest self-made women. The Forbes' international rich list has listed Winfrey as the world's only black billionaire from 2004 to 2006 and as the first black woman billionaire in world history. In 2014 Winfrey has a net worth of more than 2.9 billion dollars.

Source:

Adapted from https://www.biographyonline.net/humanitarian/oprah-winfrey.html

Discover why you are born and achieve it before you die

Ephesians 2;10- *For we are God's handwork, created in Christ Jesus to do good works, which God prepared in advance for us to do.*

1
THE CHAMPION

"Do not go through life without leaving a kind of positive mark"

Chapter 1

THE CHAMPION

You must be an uncommon man to become a champion in life

Who is a champion, and how can a champion be described? The Oxford Advanced Learner dictionary defines a champion as "an ongoing winner ...." An ongoing winner implies a winner with continuous winnings. The dictionary further describes a champion as "as a person who has been selected to represent a group of people or nation in a contest." and "someone who fights for a cause or status." Most times, when the word champion is used, the context is when there is a war, battle, a competition, a need to choose the best or the outstanding in different spheres of life. Being a champion doesn't mean you are the best in all but that in a particular aspect of life, you stand out among several other bests. So, conveniently, a champion is described as the best of the choices when set together. We have seen champions in families, in communities, in a nation and in the world at large, but remember that champions are the best in their areas of strength, and they excel and are favored beyond all in such areas.

Champion is the word also used to describe men who have attempted great things and in their attempts have found better ways of getting things done, a new cause. Champions are men of great achievements. Champions are forever recognized and celebrated for their contributions to the lives of others, communities, nations, and the world as a whole. Champions are men of territorial influence and affluence.

The word and meaning of champion have been misconstrued in many ways. Conventionally, a champion is anyone who excels above equals or mates in a competition or any course, as the case may be. The Bible and other relevant historical books beg to differ. While in the conventional view, a champion is seen to be someone that excels and succeeds above others in one thing, this is not the case from the greater biblical point of view, which considers a champion as actually succeeding in all things. This implies that the champion's title is not limited to athletics or sports, or some course or personal achievement. The real championship starts from personal life, extending to family life, and every other aspect of life.

In the Bible, and over the course of history, we have seen and read about several champions that we can truly identify with: Our Lord Jesus Christ, Abraham, Joshua, Jacob, David, Paul the Apostle, Mother Theresa, Nelson Mandela, Abraham Lincoln, Dr. Martin Luther King Jr. and so on. These champions mentioned above are not just historical figures, but people other champions look up to as role models. We can safely explain in details who a champion is using the lives of these champions mentioned above.

One of the most remarkable things about any of the champions mentioned above is that they all began as ordinary people and slowly won victory after victory that finally ensured their place as champions. They were not born champions (except our Lord Jesus Christ). But, slowly walked their ways to become champions; and in doing so followed a road map that is consistent with championship, a road map that allows you to understand who a champion is, and a road map that if followed and applied in your life, will make you a champion too.

> **You don't get to be world champions without a struggle-** *Eric Cantona*

Olympics, the most significant sporting event on the planet, lasts no more than three weeks but takes four solid years of preparations in terms of finance, efforts and time. Countries spend a lot to prepare their athletes. Four solid years for a 3-week event is not a joke! The question is, why would a nation decide to give so much and for so long for such a short-time event☐Why would countries in the face of severe economic crunch, squeeze out so much money to sponsor their athletes? The answer is not farfetched. There can be no better way to showcase the best of a country than showcasing the champions of that country. A country of champions is valued above any other thing in the universe. It is the envy of every nation. Neither individuals nor nations cherish either defeat or loss.

The pain and shame of defeat are worse than anything. Conquered or defeated nations could face the consequences as dire as losing their identities. Such could be the extent a defeated one could go. Most times, the names of individuals are what could be used to remember or attach importance to a country. Usain Bolt, Carl Lewis, Evander Holyfield, Babe Ruth, etc. are wonderful names from Jamaica and the United States, but as popular as these countries might be, it might surprise you to hear some people telling you that they only know the countries from the name of the Champions they possess. Since the word champion leaves an overwhelming sense of joy and awe, what then can we say a champion is?

> **The quality of our lives depends to a large degree, on the outcome of our decisions**

From the perspective of the Business Dictionary, a champion is a "Person who voluntarily takes an extraordinary interest in the adoption, implementation, and success of a cause, policy, program, project, or product. He or she will typically try to force the idea through entrenched internal resistance to change and will evangelize it throughout the organization. A champion can also be called a change advocate or a change agent.

When that definition is critically looked at, an essential thing to be taken from there is determination. It states that the person takes an extraordinary interest. It further emphasized the use of force. The word champion is never used when there is no determination. An effort is applied. There are so many inventions that have mocked superstition and liberated humanity: the steam engine, the spinning wheel, the airplane, medicine, the internet, etc.

They were never inventions that came from comfort. They came from the discomfort of the times and the need to correct it. But what you are going to note here is that this discomfort had been there before the change agents took time to see to their end, meaning that, the society at that time lacked such champions. The generation of those that tried, who knew that without trying, failure was quicker than when they tried, held on and freed the universe. When Black Death (Bubonic Plague) plagued Europe, it lingered because of the lack of the will to try.

The assumption was that it had been ordained and as such, they should live with it. When solution later came from those with similar physical characteristics, except the will, as those who neglected the chance, the struggling and never-ending cycle of fear was lifted.

A champion knows that to be a champion, fear must be conquered. However, conquering fear has never been easy; to change a prevailing belief is never easy. Human beings are used to their present state. The sense of delusion that everything is in shape will be there until someone comes in, or something happens, to change the situation.

● To live our dreams we must wake up

When David, in the Bible, was faced with the most challenging situations of his life, he was left with no other option than to bring his champion ability to bear. The Philistines came after the Israelites, who were gripped by fear when they saw the size of their warrior, Goliath. They lost all hope of engaging in a war. Goliath was not only a fearless and experienced warrior; he equally had the size and power to wage war against any opponent. David arose like a champion and came to the rescue. David was also human, and fear would have at first held him down (1 Sam 17 NIV). Of course, David would not have been taken as a warrior- he had never seen battles, but he had the intellect and mind of a champion. Of course, he was rejected to face such a fight, but he was determined.

No sensible human would have advised David at first fight to face a monster like Goliath. Were Goliath just a fighter steeped in his tactics alone, that would have been different, but Goliath was a most boastful and brash fighter. He bragged with everything. And who would doubt Goliath when he had all the endowment and was never a second best. He was the best of the Philistines, and that was it, and a boast from the master archer or spearman would not be taken for granted; he was not joking. He must have seen, engaged, and conquered so many enemies. He must have commanded fleets that rendered the opponents inconsequential and fallible. Goliath, with his savvy and frame, would have torn human beings like rags, yet he thought that the accolades and victories he had won over the years had come to be a symbol of his artistry, and would always be. David, like every young man, just preparing to face life, would have at the very sight of Goliath, either surrendered shamefully and had himself and his people be taken as captives, or be squandered from such submission. He could have run away if his chariots could do that faster than Goliath. What did David do, he conquered his fears.

> **Had the dinosaurs, in their intimidating and menacing posture, been ready to take up the task; had they made up their minds to wake the champions in them, and never relied on their physical endowment alone, their generations would have lived forever. But, when in their assumed royal status as lords of creation, they decided to see everything from that position of "it has always been there, changes are not necessary," they have now become subject of history, studied in books and observed in museums. They have ceased to exist on the surface of the earth! They had all attributes of champions, but were never perturbed to make anything out of themselves.**

The champion he was made of came to the fore, and immediately, he stood his ground and oiled his faith in God. First, the champion in him caused him to stand without doubting what the outcome of the fight would be. A champion knows what is in his inside and believes firmly in it. He knows that nothing outside gives him a chance to fight. David stood no chance in every external ramification. His arsenal was just a sling and some stones. He was not clad in any war attire that could protect him to any degree.

On the other hand, Goliath, with all his physical allure and entrapment, was heavily decked for war. He was protected. He had the best spear, and among other things, his psychologically demeaning boast.

One thing we must understand at this point is that David did not start knowing what he could do at that instant. No, he knew long before then that he was equal to any champion; Otherwise, he wouldn't have projected himself for such a fight. Although at first, they doubted him, David never doubted himself. All the standard armor or uniforms of war that were brought to him proved more to be for his loss than his win, so he discarded them. He had known long before then that he was decked inside, even when nothing would show outside. He pursued the daunting challenges like a champion.

> **Be strong and courageous. Do not be afraid or terrified because of them, for the Lord your God goes with you; he will never leave you nor forsake you."** *Deuteronomy 31:6*

Had David agreed that he should take time to prepare physically, Israel would have had a very different story, which generations coming would have heard about and shaken their heads in shame. It is safe to say that David had had a long spiritual preparation. Challenges do not wait or inform anyone, but champions take on challenges without delay. They work out their resolve to win. When the war was over, and the sprawling size of Goliath was all over the length and breadth of the field, the news went through every space to every territory that in Israel lived one simple but an indomitable champion, called David. Yes, David had believed he could do it. His firm conviction created a strong faith in God (Psalm 89:19). He knew that a champion is one who believes in making things to happen, even amid doubt and ridicule.

God does things in an unexplainable way. The resolve of champions most times cannot be rationalized, but they believe, just like David did against all the odds, that it is possible. God and champions work together because God works with those that work with conviction even when they have not seen any results. They have hope even in exceptional cases. They remain faithful. When occasions call for action, they don't fail.

We also have an example in Elijah. The story of Elijah and the prophets of Baal is a very popular one. Can you imagine one man standing against a multitude of antagonizing and sinister prophets? Before four hundred and fifty prophets boldly displaying and brandishing their prophetic call by naming the exploits of their deity and how anyone that dared to challenge them would be put to shame. Elijah stood his ground (1 Kings 18:20-40 ESV). He was convinced about his God and committed to His calling, so he was not moved. The champion in Elijah made him face these prophets. Elijah was the one that went to them. Even if you are a strong warrior, going to someone's stronghold, his empire, his kingdom or house, to oppose him, it is not an easy task; sometimes, that kind of bold decision is frowned at in the military circle.

The outcome might not be favorable or destructive. It is like going to a vast army that is very much ready for combat and boasting before them to face you, a lone soldier. Anyone that could do so must have an inexplicable sense of confidence, which is the champion in the person. Elijah beard the lion, if you can say, right in their den. Even from the spiritual angle, it is very well known that the prayers of a single, faithful person are far less than when it is done in a group. True to his conviction, Elijah defeated Baal and its prophets, regardless of their number.

Noah, Abraham, Moses, Elijah, John the Baptist, Apostle Paul, etc., were all definitions of champions. They had come to symbolize what a champion is. This implies that a champion is like every other person, who goes ahead, amid everyday experience, to change things for good by putting in extra efforts and staunch faith. Occasions and events define a champion.

Marconi, the Italian inventor, was credited with the invention of wireless telegraphy. If you can talk on handsets or wireless phones and listen to programs from around the world in the comfort of your home, then you will know what a bleak world or life would have been without a champion like Marconi. When you read the pages of your books, probably written and published abroad or very close to you, and you can comfortably carry them anywhere because they are handy, then you will know the essence of the champion we have in Johannes Gutenberg. He not only invented the mobile printing system, but he was also the first to print the Bible.

Without Noah and the meticulous way he followed the instruction to building the Ark, the human race would have been wiped out.

Yes, had the dinosaurs faced with similar catastrophe been inclined to be champions, they would not have gone down forever. Noah had a choice, and that was either to ignore or accept God. But he accepted, and our race was preserved. Jesus Christ had the opportunity to let the cup pass him by but with the boldness and audacity of a champion, he held forth the cup, and here we are enjoying the salvific privilege. Had Moses neglected his duty, the Jews would have died in a foreign land which they had always opposed.

A champion does not just start winning external battles; a champion starts by overcoming the four S of life: sin, self, Satan, society.

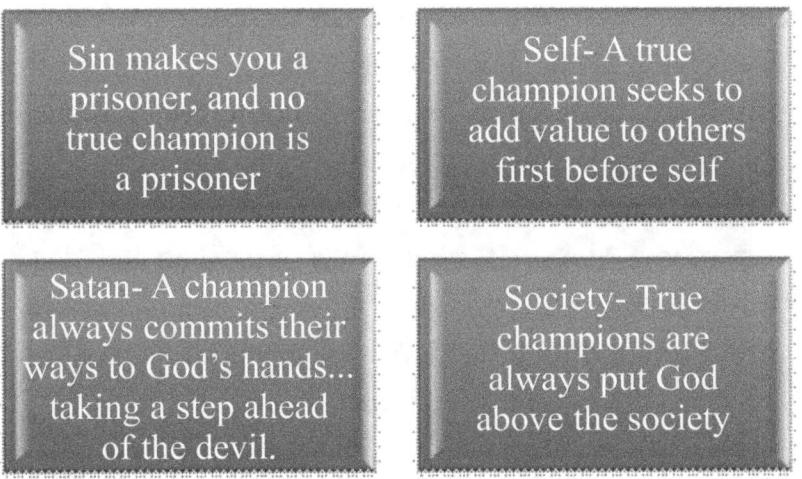

Sin: No matter the price and medals you win, and no matter the glory you achieve, without conquering the power of sin over your life, you are less than a champion. Sin is a personal enemy that reduces Victory, no matter how big that Victory is. Sin makes your victories look small, and because of that, makes you less than a champion. Because of sin, a lot of champions have fallen, and some never reached their final destination.

Self: Self in the purest form of explanation means your inclination, proclivities, and desires. A lot of people are slaves to themselves either through certain addictions or their habits/behaviors. A true champion conquers self because without overcoming self, you will always be a prisoner to you, which is very dangerous.

A lot of champions in the Bible had this challenge but had to work and pray towards overcoming it. David had a problem of self, he could not control his urges and desire for Bathsheba, and this led him to make so many mistakes. Achan too could not control himself, and he disobeyed God's commandment when he took from the treasures God said no one should touch. Even though the Israelites emerged champions, Achan did not live to tell the tale. Samson too had a strong desire he could not control, this eventually brought him down. Self is what makes you selfish, self-serving, self-centered, self-preserving, self-bias, self-inverted, self-willed, self-admiration, etc. All champions first had to deal with themselves, to be a champion you must first conquer yourself. As Solomon wrote in Proverbs 25:28, "A man without self-control is like a city broken into and left without walls."

Satan: The Bible says in 2 Corinthians 2:11 "…in order that Satan might not outwit us. For we are not unaware of his schemes." Here, the Bible warns that apart from what we see and experience physically, there is also a spiritual battle; that is why David, having learned from his mistakes said in Psalm 37:5 "Commit everything you do to the LORD. Trust him, and he will help you." During the reign of David, the devil got the upper hand on one occasion, and this brought disaster upon the children of Israel. In 1 Chronicles 21:1, "Satan rose up against Israel and incited David to take a census of Israel." Here we see David deciding without consulting God, a decision that ultimately proved fatal for both David and the children of Israel. This we see in verses 11 and 12;

> **"So Gad went to David and said to him, "This is what the Lord says: 'Take your choice: three years of famine, three months of being swept away before your enemies, with their swords overtaking you, or three days of the sword of the Lord—days of plague in the land, with the angel of the Lord ravaging every part of Israel.' Now then, decide how I should answer the one who sent me."**

The Lesson and message here are simple; Satan deceived David to take a census of Israel, which annoyed God. A champion always commits their ways to God's hands, and they run every decision they make by God through prayers, and that way, they are still a step ahead of the devil.

Society: Most champions are usually defeated by society before they become true champions. An excellent example of this is the life of King Saul. Saul was chosen and anointed by God to become the king of Israel, but because Saul decided to please the society instead of God, he fell from Grace. Saul was always conscious of "what will the people say☐" "What will my men think☐" instead of "what God will say?" or "what will God think?". This is shown in 1 Samuel 13 where Saul not only disobeyed God but ordained himself prophet by performing sacrifices that were meant for prophets alone, all this he did because he wanted to please his men and the people; his fall followed quickly. Paul told Agrippa in Acts 26:19b that "I was not disobedient to the vision from heaven." True champions are always faithful to God, to walk this path, you must learn to put God above what society, peers, friends, and family.

After overcoming the 4 S discussed above, a champion can then be identified through the following systematic victories. Remember, the road to being a champion is not completed in a day, or a year or even ten years; it takes a whole lifetime. That's why a champion should focus on taking one step at a time, one victory at a time until the war is won. Thus, a champion is someone who through overcoming the 4 S, wins;
- Personal Victory
- Family Victory
- Territorial Victory (physical and spiritual)

Personal Victory: Personal Victories for every champion starts from within. That's why a true champion first conquers the man within, before going out to defeat the enemies without. Solomon too recognized this in Proverbs 16:32 that it is better to be "one with self- control than one who takes a city."

The importance of personal Victory to who a champion is is unmatched, that is why this step is not only vital to a champion; it is a matter of life and death. In Numbers chapter 13, Moses sent 12 men to spy on Jericho and bring back reports on the lay of the place and how the Israelites might be able to conquer them. These men were all outstanding men, who were considered champions and chosen from the 12 tribes of Israel. However, at the end of the mission, we discovered that it was only 2 out of the 12 that were true champions, who had first gained personal victories before opting for other kinds of victories.

The additional ten still had personal fears; they still had shakable faith, they were not yet sure of their stand with God or what he can do for them, they did not understand their purpose and the role God played in it. Their paradigm to life was wrong, and this cost them their lives. Because when they came back from Jericho, instead of sowing the seeds of hope and courage, they planted that of fear and distrust, which cast a shadow of doubt on the children of Israel. They were carried away by the tall walls and giants of Jericho and thus believed within them that it was impossible for them to defeat Jericho. But Joshua and Caleb had a different view, which was oriented in faith and trust in God because they had built their faith in God. They had defeated their fears; thus, they had nothing to fear about the giants or tall walls of Jericho. They returned back with a favorable report, and because of Joshua and Caleb's positive attitude, Joshua was eventually chosen to lead the Israelites to the promised land.

Family Victory: A champion after achieving personal Victory must also win the family victory. A champion should also learn to be a champion in his/her home. The Bible talks about creating balance and unity in Mark 3:35 when it emphasized that "If a house is divided against itself, such a house will not be able to stand." Through this, we understand that a champion must be able to create balance and unity at home, and at the same time provide for their needs which is not limited to only financial obligations, but also spiritual, emotional and physical. Because, "if anyone does not provide for his own, and especially for those of his household, he has denied the faith and is worse than an unbeliever (1 Timothy 5:8)."

Territorial Victory: When God calls anyone, and the moment a person is born into this world, that person is either called or born with a purpose, and that purpose comes with the territory. To have territorial Victory is to fulfill the calling and purpose of God in your life. Territorial Victory comes in two forms, that is, physical and spiritual victories

Physical Victory: David and Samson are two great examples of champions who won physical territorial victories based on their calling and purpose. Samson was marked to be a champion even before he was born, and David was anointed to be a champion, but both of them had a similar purpose, which was to save the children of Israel from the oppression of the Philistines. In Judges 13:5b, the Lord prophesied concerning Samson saying, "He will take the lead in delivering Israel from the hands of the Philistines." And to David, the Lord said in 2 Samuel 3:18 "By my servant David I will rescue my people Israel from the hand of the Philistines and the hand of all their enemies." Their purpose was clear, "save the

Israelites from Oppression" and doing this meant winning territorial victories for Israel.

Spiritual Victory: Our Lord Jesus Christ and Paul the Apostle are also two people who were chosen and called to win spiritual Victory. Jesus Christ was chosen to gain spiritual Victory over all the powers of this world, and Paul was chosen to gain spiritual Victory by spreading the good news of the word of God. Both Jesus and Paul had a similar purpose, while Jesus was born to save the world from sin; Paul was called to carry this message to the world. In Matthew 1:21 the Bible says concerning Jesus "She will give birth to a son, and you are to give him the name Jesus because he will save his people from their sins." And concerning Paul in Acts 9: 15, 16 "Go! This man is my chosen instrument to proclaim my name to the gentiles and their kings and the people of Israel. I will show him how much he must suffer for my name."

A Champion ultimately takes others to Victory: All the champions I used as examples, after winning personal, family and territorial victories led many others to Victory; they added value to the lives of many people. David led the children of Israel to Victory against their enemies; by ensuring the people lived in peace, he added value to their lives. Joshua brought the Israelites to the Promised Land, giving them a place to call home, thereby adding value to their lives. Our Lord Jesus added the most value by saving us from the power and punishment of sin and then making us heirs of God's glorious kingdom. Great figures like Rev. Martin Luther King Jr., Nelson Mandela, Mother Theresa, and General George

Washington all added values to people's lives by leading them to personal, family, and territorial victories.

God's call for you to be a champion takes different dimensions and can affect your life in different ways. His calls can take you through a rough patch, but that rough patch might just be meant to mold you into the kind of champion God wants you to be. You may be going through certain hardships and struggles in your life; life might not be as you want it and it may appear as if your whole world is falling apart, then you should not be discouraged because hardship and endurance are all parts of what God will use to take you to your destination. It is all part of God's plan, whether you are successful or whether you fail, God is taking you somewhere. Remember it does not matter who wins the battle, what matter is who wins the war. General George Washington lost more battles than he won, but in the end, he won the fight by using his leadership to help secure America's independence. So, understand this, God has a plan to make you a champion, and that plan includes all you are passing through right now.

Many people had lived without anybody knowing their contributions. They only followed the cycle of events and consumed what others produced. They only believed that the wind of events should carry them whenever and wherever it went. But remember, the wind does not always blow in the direction we want it. And we cannot determine when the wind will start and stop. That is, living a chance-life. For others, life is for creativity and manifestation. They tried until they were able to better the world. They created schools, cars, industrial plants, household equipment, and a host of others. When you look at the wonders around you, then the likely questions will be, 'had these things not been created, what would life have been like?' 'How do you define the world without what has come to give it a form?' The world would have been a living hell. The Champions that have existed and are still existing gave us the wonders and the beauty of the world.

A Champion is a warrior fighting a war, a champion fights many battles, wins some and loses some, but ultimately a champion wins the war. A champion is not perfect, and a champion understands his imperfection and is willing to learn from their mistakes.

A champion is a David that begs for forgiveness after he discovers he has offended God, a champion is a Paul, who though started as an oppressor of Christians, makes a U-turn when he encounters Christ and learns of his wrongs, a champion is a Samson who made mistakes after mistakes but never gave up till the end of his life, a champion is a Ruth who looked beyond the now into the glorious future of vowing loyalty to God, a Champion is a Joseph who even when sold to slavery by his own brothers, thought it not right to offend God, a champion is a Nelson Mandela who suffered 27 years in prison, but still had the heart to forgive and let go. The world needs champions, and you can join the chariots!

Daniel

The champion that dared to be different, putting God first. He was determined and focused.

In the third year of the reign of Jehoiakim, Daniel and his friends Hananiah, Mishael, and Azariah were among the young Jewish nobility carried off to Babylon following the capture of Jerusalem by Nebuchadnezzar, king of Babylon. The four are chosen for their intellect and beauty to be trained in the Babylonian court, and are given new names. Daniel was given the Babylonian name Belteshazzar while his companions are given the Babylonian names . Daniel and his friends refused the food and wine provided by the king of Babylon to avoid becoming defiled. As a result, they received wisdom from God and surpassed "all the magicians and enchanters of the kingdom." When King Nebuchadnezzar had a dream only Daniel was able to interpret it: When Nebuchadnezzar's son, King Belshazzar used the vessels from the Jewish temple for his feast, a hand appeared and wrote a mysterious message on the wall, and again only Daniel could interpret the handwriting. When new king, Darius the Mede ruled, he appointed Daniel to a position of high authority. Jealous rivals rose up to destroy Daniel with an accusation that he worshipped God instead of the king, and Daniel was thrown into a den of lions, but an angel saved him, shutting the mouth of the lions; his accusers were destroyed, and Daniel was restored to his position.

Source: Adapted from the Bible- Daniel Chapters 1, 2, 4, 5 and 6

> "What does it take to be a Champion? Desire, Determination, Concentration and will to win
> - Patty Berg"

***2 Timothy 4:7** -I have fought the good fight, I have finished the race, I have kept the faith.*

2
ROAD MAP TO CHAMPIONSHIP

"Success does not come to you ..... you go to it" - Unknown

Chapter 2
ROAD MAP TO CHAMPION

"Even if you are on the right track, you'll get run over if you just sit there" -Will Rongers

Beauty does not make you a champion, height does not make you a champion, size does not make you a champion, geography does not make you a champion, sex does not, but you have the power to make yourself a champion. The world was handed to man unrefined, yet the daunting picture of refinement and crudity never removed the spark to start what has come to be known as civilization. When the early man ruled the cosmos, he was not content with the situation around, so he never folded his arms to watch. He knew that accepting the status quo would be a limitation that could make his generation not to stay long on the face of the earth, so he scratched his back, stretched himself and began the journey to civilization, in the face of the limiting and equally harsh conditions around him.

> **The true test of a champion is not whether he can triumph, but whether he can overcome obstacles- Garth Stein**

From fruits gathering (of course he would fight savage beasts), to the discovery of fire, a very remarkable discovery, man has discovered his inbounding talent. His food had come to taste better than before, courtesy of cooking and roasting with fire. He was not content with that, he drew pictures on the wall of the cave, thus showing some sense of aesthetics. He continued until he discovered settled agriculture. From that point, development exploded, and today the world has been transformed.

Without that simple but determined step, perhaps man would equally have shared the fate of the dinosaurs. But if you should ask me, "who would have told our unrewarding and spine chilling story?" Perhaps some good story tellers might have been made out of the rest of the creation that would have survived.

The beautiful things you see today that you aspire to get were not there at a time, but some people, encased in this skin that you and I share, who were not content with life as it was, brought out the champions in them and gave us those wonders. When you go to Paris, New York, London, Rome etc., what do you go to see? You see the sublime and relentless spirit of beauty created by champions. Then why not become a champion? You can be, but be ready. Are you ready now?

- **Be ready**

Bill Clinton was born like every other human being, the elements of nature during his birth were not different, the earth has revolved this way from time immemorial, there have always been day and night, as there will always be; but Bill Clinton in the midst of this everyday happenings, stood out. While Bill Clinton shared these common attributes with others, he equally had a conviction. He had the desire- the desire for the uncommon but achievable, with zeal and focus. When President J F Kennedy shook hands with him in 1963, as a member of the American Legion Boys Nation, he never took his hand shaking with President J F Kennedy the way others in his company did.

His mind went differently and he prepared for the outcome. Bill Clinton, moved by the sight and grandeur of President J F Kennedy, wrote the letters of determination on his mind and aspired from that moment to be the President of the United States. With the light of aspiration burning fiercely, and his ideas intact, he went through the common path of being the boy living within the neighborhood, playing around and doing the common chores, to attaining the uncommon, becoming the President of the United States.

Bill Clinton, at that very instant he nursed the idea of becoming the President of the United States, must have lived in the midst of some deafening noise of opposition and obstacles. He would have been queried and reminded of those that embarked on such journeys and failed. They might have shown him the grave of those that ventured and not only failed, but died with their families left to bear the brunt.

> **Despite what would seem to be a semblance of setbacks, Bill Clinton emerged strong and overcame problems that would have arisen, and in no distant time, he saw himself sitting down as the president of the United States.**

When the young Alexander controlled and rode the difficult Bucaphalus with ease, his father looked him in the eyes and said "this boy will be great". True to this, he became Alexander the Great and ruled an entire empire. These characters, whose names have come to stay, had removed the spirit of doubt. If Joseph had been a doubter, he would never have been a champion in Egypt. He rose from obscurity to fame. He rose to rule the biggest empire of his day. If he never made up his mind to be a champion, he would not have agreed to run from Potiphar's wife, rather, he would have slumped morally and spiritually. He would have lost the direction of God, and it is only a champion that can worship and follow God faithfully (Gen 39-40).

Jesus exclaimed that the Son of Man has no place to put his head even when animals still boast of having such (Luke 9:58). Such an expression would not elicit joy, but a sense of hardship. But there lay the champion- the spirit to forge ahead in the face of challenges. Doing something new from what has not been or modify what has come to be accepted as normal.

Peter was touched by the Lord and he acted faithfully and did extraordinarily. He would not have known that he would lead the apostles. But when you look into Peter's life, you would understand that he had prepared himself for leadership position. He was bold and ready to ask questions. He was very much ready to face anyone. He was very much ready to sacrifice. He knew from the start that being a champion was far more than just a local fisherman.

● Think differently, remove doubt

Peter and the other fishermen among the apostles were not the only fishermen present at the time Jesus saw them, but with the benefit of hindsight and fortitude, which a champion carries far ahead of others, they were able to receive the savior. When the message of the prophets drew near, it was not only the apostles that had the opportunity to see the Messiah at the Sea of Galilee. There would be countless others that would have been available at the sea, but they lacked the foresight and the urge of a champion. When the apostles exclaimed, "we have found the Messiah," many others around would have heard, but they were probably occupied with the present.

● You need foresight

Human dreams are oiled and nurtured with ideas and foresight. Had the world, say like five hundred years ago, been told that human beings would one day fly in a flying machine, that is airplane and other associated machines of flight, not many would believe, and among the few that would have believed, it would be to have avoided being labelled dream killers. Deep down in the corner, probably a dark spot, the idea would have been laughed off by some among the few who believed. They would have merely supported the idea just so they could have one foot in but able to easily switch ground should the idea fail. If the those that lived during the pre-airplane age were to see the present, they would have marveled at the beauty and ingenuity of such seemingly foolish idea at the time. Therefore rise above what is present and think ahead of time.

> **The idea of the present, and not the future, has been the greatest killer of would-be champions (Matt 4:18), so think ahead of time.**

Are Champions Made or Born?

A champion could come from a line of champions but he should not rest and watch because his champion's spirit or power may not manifest. A look at the non-hereditary leadership shows that only few in history succeeded their parents. Well, Emperor Augustus succeeded Julius Caesar and did very well, but he had an ambition and pursued it. He was not given the mantle of leadership on a platter of gold. He fought his way to greatness. Therefore, he became a champion by efforts and determination, and not by being in the midst of champions without doing anything.

> **Most times, hereditary leadership is fraught with errors and problems because it breeds**

Leadership has been a strongly contested position; it has never been a place for the weak-hearted. It was never meant for the lily-livered but for those that have zeal and foresight.. When Cosimo de Medici reigned in Florence, he was very effective and he brought strength and coordination, but his son Piero di Cosimo de Medici was rather weak and the administration almost crumbled. It was revived again when Lorenzo the Magnificent, his grandson took over. It was during his reign that there came the explosion of aesthetics and the birth of many artists and culture connososiers. Although Lorenzo came from hereditary leadership line, he still developed his own views and ideas. Then, he relentlessly pursued them. Today his name stands tall above any of his ancestors.

When Solomon ruled Israel very well such that there was no trouble, peace ruled everywhere. Solomon was firm and efficient in handling the issues of administration. He mastered the art of leadership. He was prepared for the challenge and he succeeded. When he died, his son Rehoboam took charge and it did not take long for the kingdom to crumble. He was not prepared for leadership because that quality of a champion was not in him. If Alexander the Great was born as a champion, he would not have been given to Aristotle for training. If peter was born as a champion, he would not have gone through long tutelage under Jesus Christ. Demosthenes achieved his feat of sublime speech through practice and nobody else was ascribed with that in his family, as an inheritance.

> **In essence, you do not have to come from the lineage of champions to be a champion, you can choose to be one by thinking differently, thinking ahead and working hard. Champions can be born and can be made. Are you ready to be one?**

The wise men in the Bible had to undertake the long journey to see the child Jesus in the manger. They knew how difficult it would be to journey from the East to see Jesus but they never held back. They were champions. There were many other Wise Men in the East at that time, yet these ones that came to see Jesus will forever be mentioned. Esther was a champion not because of inheritance or birth, but she mastered the art of reaching the heart of the king. With her mind set on the target she defied the law forbidding anyone from seeing the king at a particular time. She was able to get down to the heart of the king. This led to freedom for the Jews, even when all odds would have been against them. All these characters mentioned have trained themselves in the art of becoming champions.

They never inherited it. Although precocious children exist, yes special people exist, but they need the effect of the environment to act. It was even said that to be a genius takes one percent gift or luck and ninety nine percent hard work. Yes, a king Josiah could be born, who could be in charge at a very young age, but cases of such ability are rare. Prophet Jeremiah was a champion. He delivered the pure and uncontested message from God thus making the people to identify the false prophets. He had attacks, but they could not make him to buckle. He knew that truth denied will forever bring about a corrupt society.

Martin Luther King

Martin Luther King Jr was one of America's most influential civil rights activists. His passionate, but non-violent protests, helped to raise awareness of racial inequalities in America, leading to significant political change. Martin Luther King was also an eloquent orator who captured the imagination and hearts of people, both black and white.

Martin Luther King, Jr. was born in Atlanta on 15 January 1929. He attended Morehouse College in Atlanta, (segregated schooling) and then went to study at Crozer Theological Seminary in Pennsylvania and Boston University. While at the University, Martin Luther King became aware of the vast inequality and injustice faced by black Americans. A turning point in the life of Martin Luther King was the Montgomery Bus Boycott which he helped to promote. His boycott also became a turning point in the civil rights struggle – attracting national press for the cause, which began in a harmless circumstance on 5 December 1955. Rosa Parks, a civil rights activist, refused to give up her seat – she was sitting in a white-only area. This broke the strict segregation of coloured and white people on the Montgomery buses. The bus company refused to back down and so Martin Luther King helped to organise a strike where coloured people refused to use any of the city buses. The boycott lasted for several months; the issue was then brought to the Supreme Court who declared that the segregation was unconstitutional.

Martin Luther King was an inspirational and influential speaker; he had the capacity to move and uplift his audiences. In particular, he could offer a vision of hope. He captured the injustice of the time but also felt that this injustice was like a passing cloud. King frequently made references to God, the Bible and his Christian Faith. His speeches were largely free of revenge, instead focusing on the need to move forward. He was named as Man of the Year by Time magazine in 1963; it followed his famous speech "I have a dream" – delivered in Washington during a civil rights march.

"I have a dream that one day this nation will rise up and live out the true meaning of its creed: "We hold these truths to be self-evident: that all men are created equal." I have a dream that one day on the red hills of Georgia the sons of former slaves and the sons of former slave owners will be able to sit down together at a table of brotherhood"

Martin Luther King was awarded the Nobel Peace Prize for his work towards social justice. King recognised his oratory gift and used it to positively influence his people. After his death, and in his honour, America initiated a national Martin Luther King Day. He remains symbolic of America's fight for justice and racial equality.

Source: Pettinger, Tejvan. *"Martin Luther King Biography"*, Oxford, UK. www.biographyonline.net

> "But as for you, be strong and do not give up, for your work will be rewarded."
> *2 Chron. 15:7*

> **Every champion today was ordinary man yesterday. What they do with their hands transformed them.**

Ecc 9:10- *Whatever your hand finds to do, do it with all your might, for in the realm of the dead, where you are going, --there is neither working nor planning nor knowledge nor wisdom.*

3
PATHWAYS TO CHAMPIONSHIP

"Footprints in the sands of time are not make by sitting down"

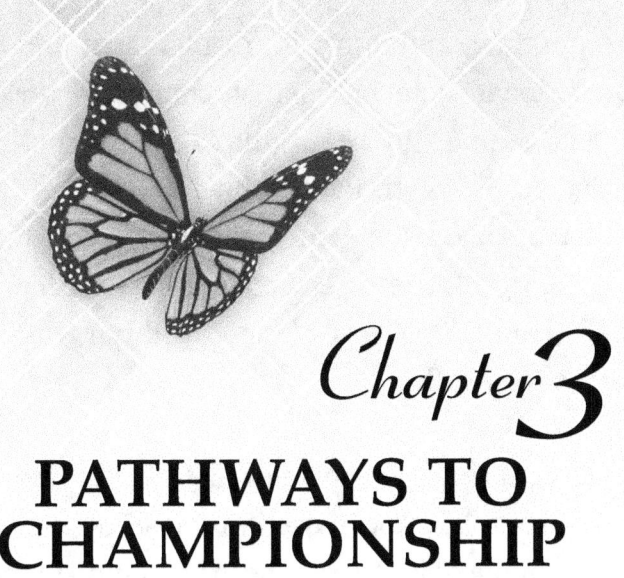

Chapter 3
PATHWAYS TO CHAMPIONSHIP

Each man has his own gift from God; one has this gift, another has that- 1 Corinthians 7:7

When it comes to championship, there are actually two clear ways to excel as a champion. While some people become champions physically, some are champions spiritually; either way, both work hand in hand to make the world a better place. It is however, important to explain their roles distinctly.

In the physical world, there are champions in various fields and endeavors. There are champions in the field of science, who lead new inventions, there are champions in the world of entertainment and champions on battlefields between nation, amongst others. In the physical world, people don't just wake up as champions, they work through thick and thin with results testifying to their feats. There can be local, state, national champion or world champions. Men like this are many in the scriptures: Abraham, Moses, Joshua, David, John, Jesus, Peter, Paul and many more and we also have those that have walked the earth in the last two centuries, like F. F. Bosworth, George Jeffrey, Lester Sumrall, Oral Roberts, Charles and Frances Hunter, Charles Wesley, Kathryn Kuhlman, Charles Parham and several others.

Overtime, and during the course of history, numerous champions have emerged and have been used in this book, as case studies to explain some of the points here. These champion in their own ways excelled in two different ways, some physically and some spiritually. For instance, Samson, as a warrior, excelled as a champion physically, he had physical strength and sagacity, but lacked the spiritual foresight to scale the murky waters that often times surrounded the herculean role of leadership.

King David too was a champion physically; he conquered Goliath, and defeated all the enemies that confronted him physically. However, David too was not a spiritual champion, and during his reign required the help of prophets to help guide most of his decisions. Some other leaders, such as Joshua, Abraham Lincoln, Esther, and Nelson Mandela were all physical champions. That means they excelled as champions physically.

Spiritual Champions includes the likes of Elijah, a man of power and faith. From his life's example we see a man with nothing but who commands so much authority, enough to stop the rain from falling. Champions who excel spiritually in most cases lack physical power and are often at the expense of the authority or those in charge. Samuel too had no army, but Saul did, yet with just a few words, Samuel was able to remove Saul from the throne when he said "The LORD has torn the kingdom of Israel from you today and has given it to one of your neighbors--to one better than you (1 Samuel 15:28)." Paul the Apostle, John the Baptist, Peter and most of the disciples of Jesus were all spiritual champions, who fought diligently for the spread of the gospel, but still met gruesome deaths because of their fight for righteousness.

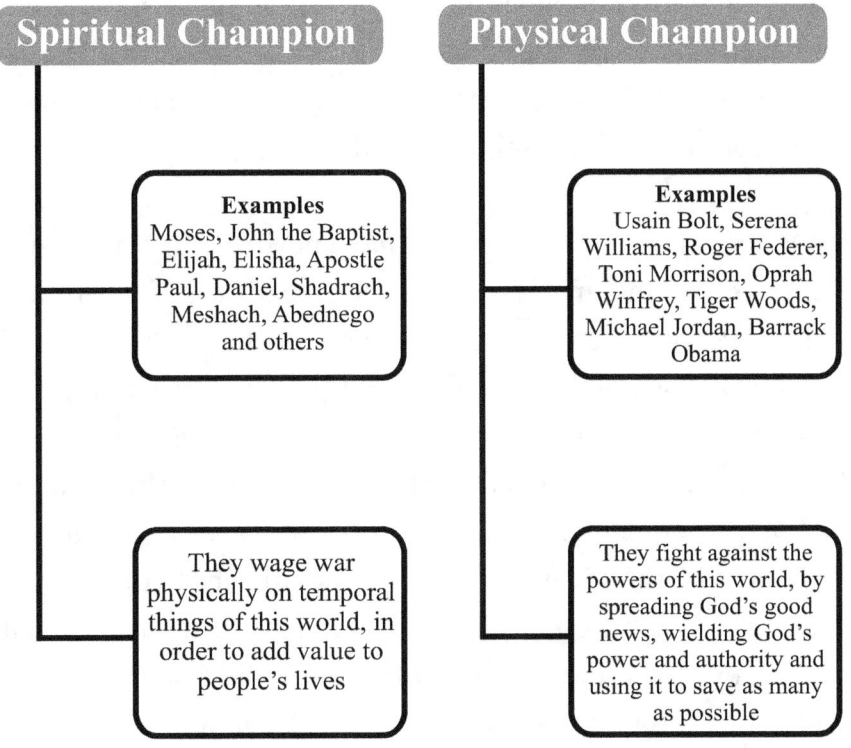

These physical champions have become household names. The mention of their names drive a sense of fulfillment and euphoria into people. They have got fans all over the world to the extent that some citizens of no few countries have come to know their names far better than those of their own leaders. They have grown to become citizens of the world and not of their countries alone. They are celebrated, and many dream to see them walk on the same earth they walked on. For some people, merely seeing them on TV is an achievement great enough. Most times the celebration does not stop, generations coming will keep hearing the exploits of these men, even when they might have long gone.. It was not that life was very easy for these ones, but they had to push through the maze of uncertainties and challenges of life, not allowing circumstances to define them. They prepared themselves for the task ahead and today their names have come to represent a shining side of humans that will continue to be a compass to others.

Spiritual champions like Abraham have performed exploits in the spirit, and down the line, left us the heritage of salvation. Abraham was like every other man in his country home but one with foresight. Had he not the mind of a champion, ready to venture into the tough and unexpected, he would not have listened to what his fathers or his ancestors never thought of. Armed with his champion mettle of discernment, he knew when Yahweh spoke; he must have discerned something different from others in that voice. He had heard voices but that one was unique. He agreed against the status quo to follow the voice. Had Abraham not heard that voice, or had he failed to follow that voice, perhaps Judaism and our Christian faith would have had a very different and hard to realize path. Again God could as well be made annoyed and this would equally have affected our course today. If God could punish Adam such that mankind came under heavy burden of sin, it could be reasoned too that if Abraham had refused to heed the call, it would likely have caused some not too pleasing effects. Abraham ventured and set out on a path that forever gave illumination and hope to mankind.

Moses, in his encounter with the burning bush, believed the voice talking him because the voice indicated that ' He is the God of Abraham, Isaac and Joseph. Abraham had sown a good seed that generations coming after will have the opportunity to follow a good path to God. One thing must not be lost, these acts to becoming champions have never been easy but they must be tried since it will liberate people in the long run. When the suffering of the Israelites in Egypt got to the high Heaven, they were not neglected because of the champion of liberation in their midst, Moses. Moses knew the happiness of royalty; he saw the privilege from being in the palace; he knew what it meant to have known or rub shoulders with the Pharaoh of Egypt. He could get everything at the stroke of his fingers. Yet, he considered the high position he had come to attain, as a downturn to his championship drive. Being aware of the pain that would follow should he reject the discomforting but liberating call from God, he risked his position and got involved. He knew that a champion was the one that would liberate his people and he endured and did what would have been impossible.

It may be argued that Moses had God by his side, but then, there were cases where God called some people and they failed God: Adam failed God, Samson failed God, and Ananias and Sapphira failed God. The angels that came down from heaven to sleep with the daughters of men failed. Lot's wife failed. These people knew God but they never had the courage of a champion.

Come to think of it, when Moses came to the Red Sea, the champion in him came to the fore, as he felt the fear and pressure from his followers. Those that had been accustomed to the old ways in Egypt would have, at that point shouted discouragingly. Some of the pessimists from the outset that grudgingly followed him would have at that point called Moses a charlatan. Just imagine what that would have done to the crowd. Moses as a champion in the heat of the storm must have felt the seeming hopelessness. Yes, champions equally see the futility of their ambitions, following the barrage of criticisms, but like the philosopher, Ralph Waldo Emerson said, 'the spark of idea that seems inconsequential carries the critical development humans would celebrate'. Thus, Moses, armed with foresight, was stretched both physically and spiritually, yet he had set his eyes on the goal like a champion would do. And when the Red Sea parted, not few eyes would have been glued to it in awe,

Again, it should be understood here that not everyone that opposes you does it out of hatred. Something that is not willful but overwhelming is perhaps at play; it can also be ignorance. Therefore, when you are determined to do something, do not listen to dissenting views, the voice of negation and long noise of fear and failure. These are the loudest voices, but they are destroyed or overcome by determination and doggedness, which are very active ingredients of champions.

> **The belief that life or things are fixed is the greatest cause of fear and failure and these two are the graveyard of the spirit of championship.**

Barrack Obama was a president of the United States and with his persuasive speeches, he got the heart and sympathy of the people. It is not that speaking was easy, no. He would have had raw moments of having to stay focused to align his speech so that he would achieve his higher aim of becoming like those that attained the highly esteemed position of the president before him. Usain Bolt knew his goal and he trained so hard. He kept on training so as to win. He remained focused. The same can be said of other champions mentioned. They knew the prize for victory. They knew that victory could not be picked just by entering into a competition. They made it a habit to keep practicing under unpalatable conditions.

Nonetheless, everybody cannot be a champion. It is reserved for those with the focus, zeal, hunger, determination. When Demosthenes knew that his chances of being a very good orator was threatened by his weak speaking power, he conceived the idea of going to the coast. He went there early and came late. He would put pebbles in his mouth and practice speaking at the top of his voice. At first it was difficult, but with time, the difficulty gave way. It is recorded that Demosthenes gave a most nearly perfect speech in history. You can get this in what has come to be his Philippics. These people believed in the physical and they went physically for it.

It is often said that the spirit controls the physical, so let us take look at the spiritual. The characters like Moses, Elijah, Daniel, among others are spiritual champions. They knew that something higher exists and they believed in its overwhelming power against the prevailing and fact supporting physical experiences. They prevailed against rationality and came out with tangible and amazing results. Let us look at the case of the "three becoming four." When Shadrach, Meshach and Abednego were thrown into the fire at the command of King Nebuchadnezzar, they knew that to live was to stick to the rules of the king, but they equally knew that it would violate their own belief, which was the belief in Yahweh.

Everything physically around them at that material time pointed to their doom. And the king would be pleased that those he would use to test his will had been found. Yes, the fire was increased four times more to serve as deterrent. But these young men defied both entreaty and warning. Eventually, they were past salvation and were deep in the middle of blazing fire , but they were resolute, as champions. They believed Yahweh. They even boasted that should Yahweh not save them, that they would be all right. It did not take long for their number to increase from three to four. Amazingly, it was the people outside the furnace that died from the heat from the furnace. The rest of the story was that of their freedom and eventual glorification of Yahweh.

Then another striking example of spiritual championship was the case of the woman with the issue of blood. She was never allowed to have access to Jesus, both by human and medical barriers. However, on the spiritual level, she was a champion; she believed that the helm of Jesus's garment would heal her. Since physically she could not touch Jesus, she spiritually exercised her daring belief and that actually saved her. The Centurion's servant was saved due to his believe because he was a champion. Yes a champion does not take the common path, otherwise, it will never be. Whether physical or spiritual you must be ready to endure and face criticism without giving up.

When Namaan came all the way to see Elisha, he was never a champion. He believed in the gigantic and magical, but he was never a spiritual champion. He was only physical. He doubted the prophet, not until his servant helped him. His servant was more of the spiritual champion. Without him, his master would have gone home not healed (2 Kings 5: 1-19).

Therefore, there exist physical and spiritual champions; while most spiritual champions affect both the spiritual and physical life, the physical champions most of the time are concerned with only the physical. The connectedness is that spiritual yields physical results too. David called on the name of Yahweh because he believed in him. That is spiritual, yet he achieved a very great physical result. Goliath fell and the Philistines were defeated and the Israelites gained their freedom.

Whatever you do, work at it with all your heart, as working for the Lord, not for human masters, since you know that you will receive an inheritance from the Lord as a reward. It is the Lord Christ you are serving.
Colossians 3:23-24

Joseph

He held unto his dreams, remained focused and faithful. He paid the price through hardship to emerge a champion.

Joseph, the favored son of the patriarch Jacob, was given into captivity by his own envious brothers. When Joseph turned seventeen, his father had a wonderful colored coat made for him that aroused the jealousy of the brothers. When Joseph was sent to a distant pasture one day to look after his brothers, they seized him, tore off his coat, threw him into a dry well and, the later sold him as a slave to traders on their way to Egypt. This was how he entered the service of Potiphar.

A tireless and highly productive worker, Joseph won his master's trust and became the steward of Potiphar's household. However, Joseph was lusted after by Potiphar's wife, who tried to lure him into her room one day. However, Joseph preferred punishment, even death, to betraying his master. So he fled while the desperate woman tore off his garment and used it as proof of her violation. Potiphar had Joseph jailed to vindicate his wife publicly. In prison, Joseph was assigned to attend two high court officials who were suspected of having stolen a bracelet from Pharaoh. Tormented by dreams, the men asked Joseph for help. Joseph told the cup-bearer that he would be reinstated while the chief-baker would be hanged. Two years later, the cup-bearer remembered Joseph when the Pharaoh was unable to obtain from his priests a rational interpretation of two disturbing dreams. Joseph was summoned and he interpreted the dream. Pharaoh thereafter appointed Joseph as his prime minister. After seven years a murderous famine drove people from nations near and far to come to Egypt to buy grain. Among the famished, Joseph recognized his brothers and tested them to see if they had changed, Satisfied that they had, Joseph revealed his identity. Finally reunited with his beloved brother Benjamin and his father Jacob, Joseph reconciled with his family, and the Pharaoh invited them to settle in Egypt as overseers of his livestock.

Source: Adapted from the Bible- Genesis Chapters 37, 39, 40 and 41

For your new you to emerge you have to change your thought

Romans 12:2- *Do not conform to the pattern of this world, but be transformed by the renewing of your mind. Then you will be able to test and approve what God's will is—his good, pleasing and perfect will.*

4

ATTRIBUTES OF A CHAMPION

If you do what you have always done the same way, you will continue to get what you always gotten.

Chapter 4
ATTRIBUTES OF A CHAMPION

*Champions never quit; Thomas Edison tried
1600 times before inventing the electricity bulb*

Abraham was promised a land filled with milk and honey. He was given the promise that he would bear a son, yet he was in his old age. He was taken away from the land of his ancestors that he had become accustomed to, yet he never questioned God. Jesus Christ left the celestial kingdom, where he was worshipped and adored with the Father and the Holy Spirit. Moses left Pharaoh's beautiful palace and the great respect it had given him, to follow the lowly children of Israel. Let's visit Abraham again. He was promised a son, and he eventually got it, but the same bundle of joy was requested for sacrifice. Abraham, just like every other human being would have experienced a shock. He must have believed that tragedy, the seven-letter word was permanent on life's notice board. He must have felt pained beyond measure. He must have felt that his generation would be gone, yet he clung to the undiminished belief in himself and his creator. Belief is a powerful tool. Had he not believed, Abraham would have failed his Maker. His belief and faith gave his generation the edge to have God on their side (Gen 22).

> **Believing in the benefit and the power of a course is a champion's helmet**

When Adam failed to believe in Him that created and organized the garden that he was benefitting from, all his offspring had to pass through the most delicate and painful dethronement caused by sin. Another important quality Abraham had was discernment. Before Abraham was called out of his father's land of Ur of Chaldeans, the worship of deities and other gods were in existence. He was not moved. Remember he was not born into a family that had known the Almighty God; after all, the worship of any such God was unheard of at the time. But Abraham's ability to know the voice of the true God was remarkable. It must be noted here that Abraham achieved a feat. He had the spirit of discernment. He had been in the midst of these deity worshippers; some would be very close friends and family members, yet he identified the true God. Lack of discernment does not allow a person to look at things wholistically or study the trends before making decisions..

> **Discernment makes a champion.**

Nothing distracts a champion from attaining his set goal. Whatever the obstacle or its semblance, s/he is undeterred. Jesus gave a very good example of how a goal is aligned by a champion. When Peter insisted that he would go nowhere, Jesus vehemently replied: "Get behind me Satan." (Matt 16:23). This shows that Jesus would not be distracted, not even by a disciple he loved, especially knowing that the devil spoke through him at that moment. Being goal oriented
is not limited to individuals alone, nations, being goal-oriented, also spend long time to prepare for Olympics; for such short events as cycling, judo and the rest that might not take more than few days to compete for.

A champion has a goal in focus

Sometimes around July, 1969, man had conquered one of the most awesome adventures he set out to achieve. A very ambitious and daunting task, yet he landed on the moon. Although this would not have ever been imagined some few hundred years before, but the relentless quest of champions made it to happen. When Moses led the Israelites away from Egypt, he was faced with the seemingly impossible task of crossing the Red Sea. With firm belief in God, the unimaginable happened- the Red Sea parted. This success was as a result of Moses' belief in possibilities. Looking at the slow pace of science and medicine during the dark ages, not many people would have believed that the present day advances would have been achieved. Some champions made it happen! Therefore, a champion's first and foremost believes that what s/he aims at will be achieved. All the feats achieved in the world have been conceived and believed in, even if they appear strange. Noah in the Bible, was directed to build an ark that would survive the flood (Gen 6:8-22). He would have imagined a lot of things that would not make it happen but he held on to the possibilities. First, a champion has to believe in the realization of his dream; if there is no possibility, there can never be attempt. Let it not be denied that these champions equally witness failures like other human beings. Their idea and the drive towards getting it to reality might have crumbled along the line, but they refused to let it be the end; the champions would rather use the lessons from such to fine-tune their drive.

A champion is never tired of dreaming about possibilities

Great sports men and women, great warriors, wonderful men and women of valor, great Christians and faithful men in history all formed the habit of winning. They all have the mentality of winning. It is habitual. The Bible says pray without season. Here the Bible implies that to be a champion, one must make praying a habit. Be it spiritual or physical, championship is habitual. You must make what you aspire to achieve a habit. This will give you the spirit of championship. Habit makes something a part of you and does not leave you. Due to the fact that Jesus formed the habit of praying, he never found anything insurmountable. He prayed both night and day. This made prayer a part of the Lord Jesus Christ, and nothing did he achieve without prayers. He knew that armed with prayer, which had become a habit, he would succeed in every way. People specialize in a field by doing things over and over such that when questions or issues about that field come up, answers, very useful ones indeed, would be given. Training is just an act to achieve perfection.

Championship is a habit

A champion is someone who has identified his passion and keeps fueling the fire of that passion. Champions are men of great exploits in an area of life because Jack of all trade is a master of none. Champions take their time while growing up to find the passion, an area where all their senses and mind function at the peak, it is what they love doing. It is the first thing that you will always find with any champion around you. Fueling that passion involves them taking note of how best to grow that passion. Where growth doesn't exist, decay sets in. They are men of deep study and research. When champions have discovered their area of interest, they equip themselves in that area. Knowledge is strength and the mastery of knowledge is transformation to becoming relevant. When the adequate knowledge of the area of keen interest is available, it opens the way to getting things done. This enables them to belief that impossibilities don't exist

Champions don't just do everything, NO!

in such area. Even though many people believe that in every area of life there are limitations, champions are defilers of this assertion because they are men of resolute opinion and motivation.

Allen Fox, Author of "the Winner's Mind" said, 'losses challenge a champion and actually increase their motivation'. With a stronger determination and intense work on themselves in preparation against their next attempts, they cross all "T's" and dot all "I's" that are expedient for the next intended victory. This is a trait you see in champions. They are men who live from the inside out. No amount of outward discouragement, disappointments and failures can debar them from taking the next step. Their inward persuasions far exceeded their outward realities. Against all odds, they go all the way to get things done. They are men that don't believe impossibilities exist, so they keep putting all their spirit, soul and body into what they set to achieve.

Principles set standard of living for champions

Champions are men of principles. Men of great exploits are men who have truly exercised themselves in different principles, fostered by great discipline.. The life of a champion doesn't permit him to just get involved in anything or anyone; hence, the way they live must be regularly looked into and pruned of every form of distractions. Looking carefully into the life of a champion, it has been observed that they are careful of what they get entangled with as what we engaged in add or subtract from our capacity.

They are men of consecrations, even like God did with Saul of Tarsus and Samson. Reading the book of Judges 13:3-5, 12-14 showed us the demand of God for a baby boy He is sending to the world as a deliverer. Consecrations like this set men aside for the use of God only, and do you know that some physical champions live by some of these consecrations too?

They are men of great faith in getting result. Their faith stirs them towards taking the right action per time as touching whatever they want to do. Exploits are not farfetched from men of great faith, who pursue their convictions with all doggedness and perseverance. The book of Hebrews 11 popularly referred to as the Hall of Fame of men of faith revealed what men did through faith and the possibilities that still lie for those that could tread their paths.

> **The faith of men characterized the exploits they do.**

In addition, champions have been known to be men who are not stagnant. Taking steps towards a goal is an inarguable character of champions. Even when you don't see them taking the steps openly, be fully aware now that they are working in the secret on how to bring forth a wonder in their fields or lives.

> **Stagnancy doesn't find room with champions.**

Barack Obama

Barack Obama was born 4 Aug 1961 in Hawaii. His father was a Kenyan intellectual and his mother a white teenager from Kansas. When Barack was still young, his father abandoned the family and Barack would only meet his father on a few future occasions. After a brief spell living in Indonesia, he moved back to Hawaii where he was raised by his grandparents.

Obama could have hidden under his unstable family background to choose the path of irresponsibility. Not Obama. In spite of the ridicule about his nationality, he forged ahead. After studying law at Harvard, he worked as a civil rights lawyer in Chicago.

Despite a lack of political experience, he put forward his name for the Democratic presidential candidate in 2008. Against the stiff opposition of Hilary Clinton, Obama ran a near perfect campaign. His campaign generated a flood of popular grassroots support, making use of social media and internet networking. Against the much older Republican candidate Senator John McCain, Obama won a hard-fought contest taking the 2008 presidential election. His victory was greeted with an unusual degree of enthusiasm and excitement – not just in America, but around the world. After decades of racism and segregation blighting American society, the election of the first black American president was hugely symbolic. Barack Obama served as the 44th President of the US from 2009 to 2017. He was noted for retaining a dignified and calm demeanor; he is widely regarded as a charismatic speaker – frequently speaking on the ideals of hope and optimism. Some of his quotes are:

> "Hope in the face of difficulty, hope in the face of uncertainty, the audacity of hope: In the end, that is God's greatest gift to us, the bedrock of this nation, a belief in things not seen, a belief that there are better days ahead." (https://www.goodreads.com/quotes/178980-hope----hope-in-the-face-of-difficulty-hope-in, 2004).

> "Change will not come if we wait for some other person, or if we wait for some other time. We are the ones we've been waiting for. We are the change that we seek." (https://www.brainyquote.com/quotes/barack_obama_409128).

Despite the hostile political environment, he was able to pass a health care bill which went a considerable way to ensuring greater universal provision. A year into his presidency, he was awarded the Nobel Peace Prize (2009) for his promise to promote world peace. Many thought this somewhat premature for occurring at the start of his presidency.

Source: https://www.biography.com/us-president/barack-obama

Do you not know that in a race all the runners run, but only one gets the prize? Run in such a way as to get the prize.
1 Corinthians 9:24

> **To get to the promise land you have to navigate your way through the wilderness**

Luke 13:24 – *Strive to enter through the narrow door, because many, I tell you, will try to enter and will not be able to.*

5

REQUIREMENTS OF CHAMPIONSHIP

"Champions decides who they want to be and act on it?"

Chapter 5

REQUIREMENTS OF CHAMPIONSHIP

"Champions aren't made in gyms. Champions are made from something they have deep inside them- a desire, a dream, a vision"
- Muhammad Ali.

It is not enough to proclaim that you are a Christian, but just like a champion, you must have something of change that people see around you that will make them see your faith as you proclaim it. By being able to show the light of Christ to others, you are already a champion, the greatest champion indeed. Let's discuss what you need to have to be a champion:

Vision, Dream & Goals

Champions create dreams because progress begins with dreams. Champions are visionary thinkers. You must know what you want to do to become a champion. There must be a game plan, vision, or dream that you must write down and visualize how to achieve. You do not need higher education before dreaming. A dream is just your cherished aspiration or ambition that you wish to accomplish at a set time. Nothing ventured, nothing gained. A dream is required to be successful as a champion. You must not only dream big, but you must dream in colors. Someone said, 'if nothing in life gives you pleasure, at least have a good dream. If you can dream it, you can achieve it'. It is not just dreaming; you must pursue your dream to become a champion. Drive your dream. Don't only dream for dream sake. To live your dreams, you must wake up. You have to be a person of your dream. The higher you set your goals, the greater will be your achievement to succeed as a champion. Go confidently in the direction of your dream. Paul states in Phil 3:14, " I press on toward the goal for the prize of the upward call of God in Christ Jesus," You too need to press on towards your goal and dream. "But as for you, be strong and do not give up, for your work will be rewarded" 2 Chronicles 15:7. The Psalmist also prayed in 20:4 – May He gives you the desire of your heart and makes all your plans be rewarded.

God tested the power in Adam when He gave him the assignment of naming all the species of living creatures in the Garden of Eden (Genesis 2:18-23). Adam was able to do the assignment successfully without any trouble because of the power in him to see the things that are yet unseen. He was not confused when naming them because he had a dreaming mind; after all, God has made man in His image. The quality of your future as the champion that God wants you to be is determined by the quality of what you see today in your dream. The word of God says, "Where there is no vision, the people perish…" (Proverb 29:18). You can only become a champion tomorrow with the dream you have today. Surely, tomorrow is in the hand of God, but then God will always give you a picture of your tomorrow as He did for Joseph, but most times the question is- did you take notice "For God does speak, again and again, though people do not recognize it" (Job 33:14 NLT). God, who made man in his image, also had a dream to make His creations at the beginning. God pronounced his dream in his words:

> **"Let us make mankind in our image, in our likeness, so that they may rule over the fish in the sea and the birds in the sky, over the livestock and all the wild animals and over all the creatures that move along the ground"**
> *- Genesis 1:26*

God saw the man in his mind before He made him. Because you are the image of God, it is expected that you have a dream and vision of what God wants you to be. You are to picture and visualize what you want to be ahead. It is only when you dream that you can make a dream come true. All champions who had great achievement must have had a dream. It is only those who dream that win. You cannot become better than your dream. Every great thing in life started with a dream. God gave you two eyes to let you know that you need the vision to move forward. What you see is where you will be. You must have a dream to achieve your dream.

If you walk with God and fear of God, He will reveal your purpose in life to you in your dream! Dreams come from God (Gen 28:10-12; Judges 7:13-14). If there is a child of God who does not dream or God does not speak to him or her in a dream at times, then that person is probably not walking with God (I Sam 28:6,15). God will never do anything without revealing it to his prophets (Amos 3:7-9; Joel 2:1-3).

Some tips to achieve your dream
- Dream big
- Let your dream be original
- write down your dream
- Visualize your dream
- Have a passion for your dream
- Decide to be successful
- Remember there will be obstacles along the way
- Find out how much it will cost to achieve your dream
- Ask for advice from experts
- Break down your dream to achievable goals
- Break down your goals to objectives
- Let your goals be relevant to your vision. Focus on what is important
- Let your goals be SMART; that is specific, measurable, achievable, realistic, and time bound.
- Take action to implement the goals step by step
- Don't wait until the situation is perfect
- Discipline and consistency should be your motto
- Do not be afraid to make mistakes

- •Stick to your goals
- •Invest in yourself
- •Ignore dream killers
- •Have mentors
- •Passion:

The Oxford dictionary defines passion as 'any great, strong, powerful emotion.' It is your desire for a purpose. The starting point of all achievements in life is desire. It is the inner feeling that drives you towards what you plan to achieve. It is complicated to succeed without passion. No doubt, passion drives great achievers to achieve greater things. It is the love that you have for what you desire.

Purpose
Your purpose is what you want to achieve with your goal. It is your purpose that will guide your dream and shape your goals. The secret of becoming a champion is the consistency of purpose. Ask yourself if what you are doing today is getting you close to where you want to be. What is your intention☐How do you channel the intention toward the dream☐Find your purpose as you strive to become a champion and hold to your purpose. In nature, nothing is done without a purpose. The Bible declares

> **"But I have raised you for this very purpose, that I might show you my power and that my name might be proclaimed in all the earth"**
> *- Exodus 9:16*

> "There was a man sent from God, whose name was John. The same came for a witness, to bear witness of the light, that all men through Him might believe"
>
> *- John 1; 6-7*

From the above passage, the purpose of John is clearly stated. His purpose was to bear witness of Jesus as the Savior, Redeemer, and light that all men through Christ might believe and be saved. Did John fulfill his purpose? The answer is yes.

> "John bare witness of Him and cried saying, This was He of whom I spake. He that cometh after me is preferred before me for He was before me"
>
> *- John 1:15*

John the Baptist fulfilled his purpose and became a champion for Christ. Are you fulfilling your purpose? Hold to your purpose. Remain rooted in your purpose and ideals, and you are on your way to becoming a champion.

Focus

You need to focus on getting to your goal to become a champion. It is with the focus that the Apostle Paul was able to continue the race in spite of the challenges that came his way. He met so many obstacles by way of both the Jewish and Roman laws, yet he did not give up but remained focused. Champions focus on the target, while losers focus on what they are going through. When you change your focus, you will change your feeling. Concentration is the key that opens doors to success. Your focus determines your success in life. When the Devil tempted Jesus three good times, after he had fasted for forty days and forty nights, Jesus knew that focus on what had brought him to the earth was necessary, he defeated the Devil those three times (Matt 4:1-11). Timothy was a spiritual son of the Apostle Paul. He had some challenges concerning his stomach. He was advised to take care of the stomach and still work towards achieving Heaven. Despite the difficulty, Timothy remained focused (1 Timothy 5:23).

Now let us take a look at where a mission could be lost due to the removal of focus. Samson knew the rules, but the deception of a woman made him lose his focus. Delilah caged the championship of Samson. He appealed to the flesh and reaped failure. He lost focus and reaped humiliation. The enemies mocked him and scoffed at his God. Judas Iscariot was never mentioned as the one that would betray Jesus. It was not even prophesied that it would be from his apostles, but Judas Iscariot, having lost focus and instead playing hide and seek, fell for it (Mark 14:16). You would understand that his loss of focus cost him everything. He lost the money, his peace of mind, and finally his life. He was already aware of the Kingdom, but he was later taken over by the power of the flesh. He thought that he could manipulate his way to glory.

You oil your hope with focus

Being focused is as important as nursing an ambition. A project like the Tower of Babel was lost when focus was lost. God made the children of men to lose their common language. Then their common aim of reaching Heaven, which was equally their focus was lost (Gen. 11:1-9). When Apostle Paul said we are not fighting mere forces and rather that we are fighting spiritual wickedness in high places (Ephesians 6:12), he gave the emphasis so that we can keep our focus on the spiritual. A Christian must, like I said before, know that applying heavenly laws on earth requires a great deal of focus. The vicissitudes of everyday events could cut off every semblance of hope. This reminds me of a wonderful thing. When you have hope, you move that hope with focus. The engine is hope while the oil is focus.

Determination (Phil 3:13-15)
Have you at a time had to do something very important when everything around you would have wanted you to do otherwise? Let's bring it closer. Have you probably from exhaustion or sickness been prevented from doing something very important, say like going up a floor to fetch your book, money, food or your clothes? A case like this calls for determination.

You might want to sleep on the bed only to discover that the bed was not done, and the sleep had gotten a greater part of you, yet you would try to make the bed. These scenarios would be overcome only with sheer determination. Determination will keep you focused. When you have determination, you keep going. When Jesus was left behind at the temple in Jerusalem, his parents never considered the distance or anything; they determined that they would look for him. When Joseph was left in Egypt with the subsequent abduction of Benjamin, Jacob determined to see his child and he was taken to Egypt. He saw his child and he saw the Israelites blossom before a wicked Pharaoh took over.

Although it was predicted that Rebecca was carrying two worlds in her womb and that the younger one would rule over the elder, but it never just came about. Jacob under the influence of his mother determined to achieve the prophecy. Let's say for instance Jacob had relented, he would not have seen the prophecy fulfilled. He keyed into the advice of his mother. Remember he almost faced the severest of the obstacles. And that was what he would not be able to alter. He used all he had in his arsenal to convince or manipulate his father, but he could not alter one. He could not change his voice. He was very much aware himself that his voice would pose a great challenge, yet he was determined. Let's say he decided to back off from fear, the prophecy would not be realized.

Determination is the wheel of a champion

With determination, you can break many grounds. When you, as a champion, face obstacles, just think of those that have achieved something wonderful; even when it seemed nothing was working in their direction. Think of the determination of the Apostles. In the heat of persecution, they preached the gospel. When the early Christians were being used like experimental objects in the hands of the leaders of ancient Rome, they never wavered. They stuck firmly to their belief. (Isaiah 40:31). The same Rome that was the antithesis of Christianity later became the hub of Christianity and advanced Christianity to many lands. That was determination at work. They faced persecution, and through determination they conquered. Today Rome is a home to very many Christians. This came as a result of the efforts of champions. As a believer, you need to be decisive in whatever you set up your mind to do. The proof of desire is pursuit. Determination and extra amount of efforts are the difference between mediocres and champions. It takes determination to move into championship. Learn from blind Bartimaeus- Mark 10: 46-53.

Zealousness/Hunger

You can succeed at almost anything for which you have enthusiasm. You need the will to succeed in order to become a champion in any area of life. To get to the Promised Land, you have to navigate your way through the wilderness. To become a champion you must be zealous and hungry to succeed in a godly and legitimate way. You need endurance to be a champion. Joseph endures to achieve God's dream in his life. If you are not strong in the inside, you will not have strength to dominate in the outside.

The door to success is always marked "push"

You require zeal and hunger to see you through to championship.

> 'You need to perservere so that when you have done the will of God, you will receive what He has promised'
> - Hebrew 10:36

It takes a willing heart and a working hand to become a champion. You must be zealous and hungry to achieve your goals to become a champion. Being a champion does not start around you, it begins inside you.

Do you see someone skilled in their work? They will serve before kings; they will not serve before officials of low rank.
-*Proverbs 22:29*

Alice Zhang

Alice Zhang, the champion who dared to tread the path most dread to take is the co-founder of Verge Genomics.

While pursuing an MD/PhD at UCLA, Zhang was shocked to learn a fact every drug researcher knows all too well: 90% of medicines that start human studies fail. "It's still largely a guessing game," she says. Her startup, Verge Genomics, is the latest in a long line of biotechs that think merging the latest in computer science with new technologies for decoding the human genetic code can provide a solution.

Zhang's startup, Verge targets Alzheimer's and Parkinson's diseases, areas that most drug companies have abandoned as hopeless. The seven-person startup raised funds from firms like IA Ventures and Draper Associates, and assembled advisors including Alzheimer's luminary Paul Aisen, Harvard biotech guru George Church, and the chief medical officer of the biotech firm Alkermes.

Source: https://www.forbes.com/profile/alice-zhang/#e0d80554faf6

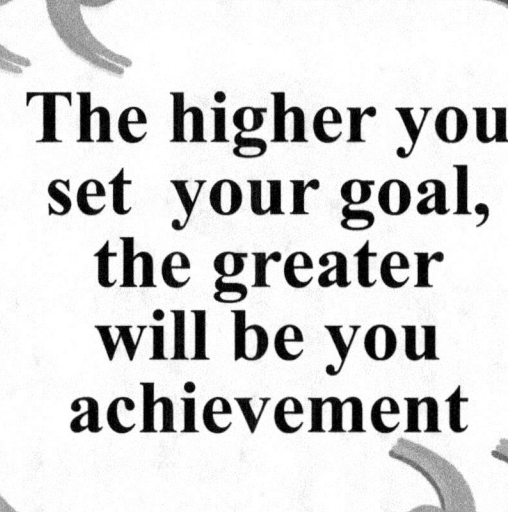

"The higher you set your goal, the greater will be you achievement"

Phil 3:14 - I press on toward the goal to win the prize for which God has called me heavenward in Christ Jesus.

6

THE TEST OF A CHAMPION

"Things turn out the best for people who make the best of the way things turn"

Chapter 6

THE TEST OF A CHAMPION

Losers focus on what they are going through, champions focus on where they are going to

The world is not an easy place. Tests are everywhere. But for you as a Christian, the world is almost a battle ground. You have to live in this world but not like others in the world. Christ has specially paid for our sins but we must be steadfast and alert. Surely, tests must come to reveal what you are made of. Elijah was tested; he was attacked by Jezebel, but with faith in God he prevailed. Peter had a challenge; he was so frustrated at the suffering of the Lord. He soon made up for his weakness. When division almost tore the apostles apart, Paul gave a very clear and humbling advice, and that is, that everyone was only an instrument towards attaining the work of the Kingdom of God. He said that Apollo, Paul and Peter were all instruments to achieving the purpose God had set.

> **It must be noted that a champion receives the greatest test.**

When Noah had finished building the Ark, he called the people to enter. He was mocked, but he never relented. Just imagine, if Noah was not a champion, he would have abandoned the Ark, just like many in his days. As a Christian, your comfort would be sacrificed for the sake of others. As a champion, the instruments of prayer and faith work wonders. When Moses was tested, first at the hands of Pharaoh, he stood his ground. Despite all the threats from Pharaoh, he never faltered. Again, he was tested at the Red Sea. He was never stopped from being a champion. A Christian is like uniformed men. They can be called to duty anytime, most times against their physical inclination. Yes it could be at the resting moment that action would come. The world is a strange place; things that turn bizarre come often. A champion could have his or her belief shaken to the foundation. Issues that have to challenge faith can be here and there. When such happens, a Christian should always stay by his conviction as did Shadrach, Meshach and Abednego. Prophet Jeremiah did it. David did it against the Philistines. Moses was not afraid to stick to his God even when the drumming power of Pharaoh was everywhere. Yes he had a life threatening challenge. The greatest power on earth in his days was Pharaoh, who was taken as half-god and half-human.

Moses knew the threats very well but being a champion he brooked no fear. He did not fret. He was even emboldened because he knew the power of the Most High would take hold and deliver him. Again

I don't know of any test that would be as tough as that of Abraham. He was childless for the greater part of his life. Then in his ripe old age, when they must have written down his name among the childless humans, he gave birth. He accepted the difficult message that he could bear a child when common sense and every factor had proved otherwise. He was even humbler in his centenary age to believe that his child would be sacrificed. An only son was to be taken away from a distraught Sarah. Her midday was turned to darkness, yet Abraham obeyed. He later came back triumphant. That was a very strong test but he succeeded because he was a champion.

Obstacles that test championship.
Pride is divisive and destructive. It destroys trust and narrows ambition. Pride keeps someone off-guard, with time will left for stock-taking and improvement. The Roman Empire got to its peak and fell from pride. They pride themselves in being able to control a very large empire, but they never had the time to maintain it. Herod was full of pride, and he lost it. For the sake of pride, Babylon was destroyed. Lucifer became proud and eventually lost his position. Humility took Joseph to an exalted position in Egypt and humility made Esther to conquer the enemies of the Jews.

> **Nothing can bring down an empire like pride.**

When Jesus was arrested, Peter lost his cool; he became afraid to the extent that he denied Jesus. Pride led Herodias to request for the head of John the Baptist. Pride led Herod to promise her anything conceivable by her. It was pride that made Goliath to curse everything about Israel. It was pride that made Jezebel to take Naboth's vineyard and attack Elijah. It was pride that made David to push Uriah to death to marry his wife, Bathsheba. Pride made the brothers of Joseph to hate and almost kill him. They sold him with hate and he bought them with love.

Fear destroys a champion.

The unwillingness to face challenges kills the champion spirit. When the apostles were with Jesus at the garden of Gethsemane, he saw how weak the apostles had become. He was frustrated that even for an hour, they could not wait to pray with him. He asked them to pray because the enemy would very soon be around. This means that a champion should be strong, whether from the spiritual or physical side of the game. There is spiritual strength and physical strength. Both physical and spiritual strength depend on training. Being focus, goal-oriented, having attitudinal strength, and the belief that you can do it will bring about championship.

This brings this issue to another side of spiritual championship. While you train physically to achieve an aim, you must arm yourself with prayers. All the spiritual champions we have mentioned were all prayer masters. Jesus himself never left the world of prayer. Therefore every other thing is secondary to prayer.

Physical championship can be enhanced by prayers. When Jesus prayed, great multitudes were fed. He used his spiritual ability to produce physical result. In everyday life, true champions are those that combine the spiritual and the physical to make the world a better place. You cannot just pray and not take action. When you lack one, you have already created an obstacle that would prevent the full attainment of your championship. When Saul lost his spiritual championship, he was troubled and eventually lost the physical championship.

> **In spite of the tests and trials, turn on your champion grit**

If there is anything that kills or filters away ambition, it is the inability to stand firm and pursue the idea. Foresight is great because with it you can raise an idea as a champion and guide it. Focus is important because you will not lose sight of your path. Determination, just like the engine of a car, continues to power a champion on. All these qualities are contained in your grit. As a champion, you combine all of these to achieve your goal. But I must remind you here that you will be the one to turn them on. Although there could be some occasions where people could help you to turn on your grit, that is, if you associate with champions, but because of the fact that you have some unique attributes, you have to develop those special areas very well because many champions exist but they exist in different fields.

If you can device newer method of evangelization such that the message of Christ could spreads fast or have people come to accept it better, then you are a champion. Learn from other champions and keep being motivated, but be unique. The world can never be tired of seeing new things but it would be tired of seeing the same thing done repeatedly. But note that you might be taught how to do something. You might be taught how to pray, how to preach etc., but nobody will put all these into practice for you. You know the best part of you that will make you a champion. You know the better time to practice and the way your body will work with specifics. Therefore cease the opportunity without delay.

Be firm in your decision. When you have grit you will not pull the brakes on the lane to being a champion even though things could test you to the limit. Again, Jesus at the Garden of Gethsemane comes into focus. When the thought and manner of his death filled him, he was filled with intense grief, such that his sweat was turned to blood. But with the grit of a champion, he never lost his sight on the mission. He endured and continued. With the grit of a champion, you can endure pain, abuse, criticism and humiliation. These are common obstacles to growth. Mockery and victimization are all means to put any blossoming idea of a champion to death but with your championship grit you are in control.

Let us look at Moses again. When God called him, he complained of having a weak or unclear voice, but he was sent. He knew the problem ahead, but he went ahead. That mission actually was a difficult one. If not for grit, it would have been impossible for Moses to go and face Pharaoh knowing what they would think of him. He was given the best care in Pharaoh's house and he was part of them, only for him to turn against them. He would have avoided such a mission, but he took up his grit of championship. Moses went there and achieved his aim. Only few leaders in history have done what Moses did, taking his country men and women away from bondage.

When the people of Israel demanded a king, Saul was given to them, but Saul never had the grit of a champion, or if he had, it lost steam. He lost out by not believing in his God, but rather went on to consult the witch at Endor. Therefore to be a champion one has to put in this grit. Saul wanted to enjoy the spoils of war. He never had the grit to overlook the good things he saw and destroy them. He did not see the better things God kept ahead of him. He was focused on the immediate. With grit, a champion conquers and reigns.

Although Jonah achieved his mission, he would not be written down as a champion. A champion cannot be dragged. Job was a finest example of a champion. He saw pain, sorrow, death and complete loss. What he struggled for crumbled before his very eyes. His faith faced the worst of challenges. His midday was turned into darkness. He mourned and it was compounded by the advice he got. But in the face of these challenges, he had very firm championship grit. He soldiered on, even when the problems seemed not to have any point of settling. He was told to curse God but did not; he praised God the more. With his champion spirit, Job was at peace with God and it did not take long for him to receive a huge reward from God. He became a famous man once again. Job was a good example of a champion who turned on his champion grit in the very face of adversity.

To be a champion in a world full of strong and smart people can never be easily achieved. So many things would come to give resistance to your movement but your grit must be turned on. You should not relent because that is where you can get the solution. As a Christian, you are a champion, but the many bizarre and unbecoming things around should not deter you, they should rather make you to know that you must put on your grit..

Something must be said here. As a champion, you may need the help of others at times. Just like Moses did as he faced the sun raising, his hands towards it. Moses got tired and others came to put stones together to support his hands. This implies that you should work in the community of those that share your ideas. As a Christian, work and share ideas with fellow Christians. Share moments together and pray together. Face challenges together and work together. The idea of supporting the two hands of Moses with stones would most likely not be Moses' idea and he eventually triumphed. A champion does not only have grit to surge forward, he equally has the grit to learn from others for improvement (Heb. 12:1).

Jessica O. Matthews

The champion in Jessica Matthews saw a need and she rose to fill the gap.

Jessica O. Matthews is a Nigerian-American inventor, CEO and venture capitalist. She is the co-founder of Uncharted Power, which made Soccket, a soccer ball that can be used as a power generator. Matthews attended Harvard College and graduated from Harvard Business School. In 2011, *Fortune Magazine* named her *Fortune*'s "10 Most Powerful Women Entrepreneurs" and in 2015, named her as *Fortune*'s "Most Promising Women Entrepreneurs." In 2012, the Harvard Foundation for Intercultural and Race Relations named her "Scientist of the Year." Matthews is a dual citizen of the U.S. and Nigeria. The President of Nigeria named Matthews an Ambassador for Entrepreneurship for the country.

She has described the inspiration for the invention as coming from an experience attending her aunt's wedding in Nigeria when the electricity was lost and diesel generators were used to keep the lights on, Matthews recognized the health hazard from the generator fumes and decided to try to do something about it. She and Silverman presented Soccket as their proposed solution, a soccer ball that stores kinetic energy when used.

In 2016, Matthews created a non-profit arm, the Harlem Tech Fund (HTF), to support 100 new startups and offer technology training to 10,000 Harlem residents over the next two to five years. Matthews serves as chairman of the board of HTF. That same year, she was recognized at the Harlem Economic Development Day, receiving the Outstanding Corporate Diversity Award. Matthews expanded to work on global infrastructure projects. She is the co-founder and executive director of KDDC, developing a hydropower dam project in Nigeria. The 30-megawatt dam is among the first hydroelectric dam projects privatized in Nigeria.

Matthews has received numerous awards, honors and recognition: Innovator of the Year by *Black Enterprise* in 2013, one of both *Forbes* 30 Under 30 and *Inc. Magazine*'s 30 under 30 in 2014 and 2016.

Source: https: // en. wikipedia . org / wiki / Jessica_O._Matthews

The higher you set your goal, the greater will be you achievement

Phil 3:14 - I press on toward the goal to win the prize for which God has called me heavenward in Christ Jesus.

7

THE CHAMPION IN YOU

"All our dreams can come true, if we can have the courage to pursue them?

Chapter 7

THE CHAMPION IN YOU

"When you want something you have never had, you have got to do something you have never done."

The world knows some opposites, which are there to check each other: the good and the bad, light and darkness, the famous and the infamous, the strong and the weak, the happy and the sad, the successful and the unsuccessful. It is a world of peaks and valleys, climax and anticlimax. Every other description hovers around them. Somebody might exist and not be known; most times, people might class him as unsuccessful or successful, depending on their measurement. Among these qualifying words, some are avoided like the plague, while others are cherished like gold. John the Baptist was a champion while Herod was a loser. Nicodemus was a champion while Caiaphas was a failure. The thief at the right hand was a champion while the thief at the left side of Jesus on the cross was a failure. The Apostles that followed Jesus till the end were champions, while the ones that fell by the wayside were failures. Ruth was a champion while Orpah was not. David was a champion while Saul was not. Jacob was a champion while Esau was not.

But you may ask why the world is so fascinated about champions. If you have walked into a place of gloom and sorrow, where the world seemed to have turned inside out, you would know that anyone that could offer some or total relief would have a crowd of followers. People spend so much to get some relief to problems. Churches give messages of hope. Christians are hope givers in the face of multifaceted issues. The miracles in the Bible were life-giving and life-sustaining. The blind man cured by Jesus was never interested in the questions the Pharisees were asking. He had found his joy. His eyes were healed.

These examples are what champions could do. Peter's mother-in-law was healed, and all were happy. Lazarus was raised from the dead. All these speak of championship. The evangelizing success of Apostle Paul in Athens was a mark of championship. He achieved the feat and paved the way for the spread of Christianity in that region. Tyndale and John Calvin, John Wesley and the rest of the reformation ministers are champions because by their efforts many realized that it is never a crime to own and read the Bible privately. Without their efforts and that of others, things would have been different.

The blood of martyrs from the days of persecution until now has oiled the growth of Christian faith. In another case, the cars we drive would not have been had there not been champions. How would life have been without cars? How would our Christian faith have been without those that faced intense attacks from the traditional leaders who felt that Christianity was a threat to their religion? The walls of Jericho were destroyed by the patient and determined march of the champions of Israel. Had they not encircled the walls against all the odds for the number of times they did, things would have continued to be against the Israelites.

Cyrus the Persian was a champion. He led the Jews to freedom from the stronghold of Babylon. He was never a Jew, so common sense would have made us believe that he would not free the Jews, but he did. Had Goliath conquered Israel, the Philistines would have ruled over them. Indeed, David was a champion. He set them free. Again, the story of the world is about champions, who did exploit. Many people would want to be known by such pleasant names as Abraham, Ruth, John, James, David, etc., but none would wish to such names as Judas Iscariot, Jezebel, Ichabod, Goliath, and Nebuchadnezzar, etc. People want to associate with something famous and good. At baptism, people would be asked to take up the names of people whose character they would like to imitate — everyone ones to associate with champions.

You should note that the world was not to be inherited but to be developed with love, faith, and hope. You must exhibit these values as a champion. You must have hope and faith. A champion does not look for personal benefit, but the benefit of others. Had Apostle Paul sought things for himself, he would have kept the word of the Kingdom of God to himself; he would not have labored all day with pains and troubles. Peter went through pain for proclaiming the Kingdom. John the Baptist was never ready to stop his preaching even when he faced the dire consequences. He never gave up.

The World is waiting for You
The world is still in dire need of innovation and improvement. The society has never been more in need than now. You are a child of God, and it is in you to make God known everywhere you go. You have the gift to say soothing words to the dying world. You could be the symbol of hope amid weaknesses and pains. You could be the voice for the voiceless. You know what you can achieve. It is in you. Do not hesitate, because Jesus never waited. For some three years and at an exceptionally young age, Jesus Christ did very well. Had David not risen to the occasion, nothing would have happened. Moses would never have been known had he not risked saving a race. Whether he agreed to take the risk or not, he would still die. He might not die or pay any price for not taking the risk, but death is for all mortals; he would still die one day. Joseph was in the house of pleasure and fame. Had he slept with Potiphar's wife, he would have earthly pleasure, but that would never save his soul or have a place for his people's interest.

When the days drew near for the word of the Lord to spread, the Apostles risked their lives, and today, we have the message of

Christ, which is our salvation. Mary Magdalene knew what she wanted. She was of the mind to hold on to the greatest gift, which was being saved from the life of sin. She held on to the one who could save her, even in the face of being taunted. She knew that Jesus was what she needed, and she never let that opportunity to go by. Nehemiah was an able administrator. He knew that the house of the Lord would be rebuilt. He did it with zeal and hope. His name is included in the list of those who were faithful to the cause of the Lord. You have the grit of a champion. If you are gifted in music, use it to help bring the Lord closer to the world. If you have the gifts to coordinate and lead, then use the gifts. If it is singing, do it to the best of your ability. Always remember that whatever you do should be done with happiness and comportment such that people would derive joy from it and give praise to God. The world is incomplete without you. There is enough vacuum because you have not contributed your quota.

You have what it takes to be a champion
You are a child of God, and with God, all things are possible. You have the power of prayer to conquer at the spiritual level. You have been initiated into the Kingdom of God. His power is above every other power. Sometimes, you could be tired and weak. There could be problems you are left to face alone. But having the power of the Most High is the greatest. It is the most important. In times like that, get to Him who made all things possible in prayer and you will survive. God will not forsake His children. He will always guide and lead them. You have *God like David to be able to face Goliath without losing any hope.*

> **The quest for improvement is in us humans, but champions do it much better**

Physical training and improvement should equally apply to you. Being a champion does not end with just living with the achievements you have made. There should always be an avenue for improvement. Always push it harder because the world has no joy when efforts are not put into it. Beautiful things are those things that came from hard work and consistent practice. Gold is never found in its raw state. It is a product of long search and persistent refinement until it attains the alluring nature it has. Gold remains to this day a most precious element. Even the Queen of Sheba was effusive with words of praise when she saw how much gold had been used to beautify the palace of King Solomon. Remember that in every competition, only one winner emerges. Therefore be very much prepared (1 Cor. 9:24). And for the heavenly race you are not a champion until the very last (2 timothy 4:7).

> **The race is not always to the swift, but to those who keep running**
> **- Anonymous**

God planted in you the seed to become a champion
We have examined God's plan to make you a champion. God takes you through certain challenges and paths that all leads to an end where you become a champion. The one thing I have come to understand about God is that, when God is taking you somewhere, or when God calls you, God always ensures that you have all you need to fulfill that purpose: he gives you spiritual backing, he gives

you physical backing, he gives you emotional inspiration and an all-round arrays of needed tools for the journey to championship. Part of the things God gives you, are the seeds necessary to make you a champion. Those seeds are in you, they just need the right soil to germinate and expand from.

Plan of God for you as a champion
God in His infinite wisdom and might exist not just as an unbeatable and undefeated being, but has replicated the capacity of a champion in His sons and daughters. God has predestined some to the life of a champion and some who came through the knowledge of Christ to God are made champions in every way. Let's take a look at the man called Samson; before his birth, God, through an angel, spoke with the father and mother on the nature of the child, who he shall become and what he is set to do with his life. The life of Samson truly depicts a champion planned by God to be undefeated throughout his lifetime. God definitely has a plan for everyone that can come to Him and the reality is that God doesn't make us less than a champion when we come to Him. Two things quickly: some are champions presently in the physical world, because it has been permitted by God, at the same time, as many that will come to God can be made to be champions for God. Why does God make us all champions? It is because His plans and vision for this earth are inexhaustible. However, it is written:

> **"What no eye has seen, what no ear have heard, and what no human mind has conceived the things God has prepared for those who love him"**
> *-1 Cor 2: 9.*

There are things yet to be seen on earth that are only accessible to believers. God wants man to have dominion on earth (Gen 1:26), this was why He created man in the beginning, but since man lost the capacity for rulership and dominion, God set another plan in motion for the restoration of man to the full glory of His vision, which gave birth to the greatest champion that ever lived, Jesus Christ. The plan of God for you as a champion could also be seen in the way He has brought your life thus far. Many times, we don't get to see the big picture forgetting that God said,

> **"For I know the plans I have for you declare the Lord, plans to prosper you and not to harm you, plans to give you hope and a future**
> *- Jeremiah 29:11.*

The plan of God for us as champions is found in the redemption package. When we give our lives to Christ, accepting Him as our Lord and personally savior, we receive the life of God, which I personally refer to as the seed of greatness in us. When we receive this life, it then depends on us either to live out this reality that is silently residing in us or die with it.

Muhammad Ali

Muhammad Ali was born in Louisville, Kentucky in 1942. He was named after his father, Cassius Marcellus Clay, Sr., (who was named after the 19th-century abolitionist and politician, Cassius. He was an Olympic and World Champion boxer, who also had a unique personality, based on self-belief and strong religious and political convictions. In 1999, he was crowned "Sportsman of the Century" by Sports Illustrated. Among several awards and medals, he won the World Heavyweight Boxing championship three times and won the North American Boxing Federation championship as well as an Olympic gold medal.

Was Ali a winner all the time☐No.

In 1993, he was beaten by Doug Jones, who, despite being lighter than Ali, beat him to the punch continually during the fight. He was also knocked down by Henry Cooper with a left hook near the end of the fourth round. However, despite these close calls against Doug Jones and Henry Cooper, Ali became the top contender for Sonny Liston's title.

In 1964, Ali failed the Armed Forces qualifying test because his writing and spelling skills were inadequate. Yet, in early 1966, the tests were revised and Ali was reclassified 1A. The champion in him refused to give up. He was beaten, but rose up to his feet, and fought again. He failed but tried again. And, when in the early 1980, Ali was diagnosed with Parkinson's disease, the champion in him chose to see the positive in the situation by saying "Maybe my Parkinson's is God's way of reminding me what is important. It slowed me down and caused me to listen rather than talk. Actually, people pay more attention to me now because I don't talk as much….I always liked to chase the girls. Parkinson's stops all that. Now I might have a chance to go to heaven."

Muhammad Ali died on 3 June 2016, from a respiratory illness, a condition that was complicated by Parkinson's disease.

Source: https://www.biographyonlinw.net/people/successful.html

"To succeed in anything, it is necessary to know the rules and understand how to apply it."

2 Timothy 2;5- Similarly, anyone who competes as an athlete does not receive the victor's crown except by competing according to the rules.

8
TURNING YOUR POTENTIAL TO REALITY

*"Work hard and prepare yourself,
then your chance will come"*

Chapter 8

TURNING YOUR POTENTIAL TO REALITY

The door to success is always marked "push"

Looking at the story of David and his encounter with Goliath, it is crucial to see how he turned an inherent capacity into a reality within some few hours. Turning your potential into reality can sometimes takes hours, days or weeks. The law of process is set for every man to bring them up to a standard where they can be actualized. Before your reality can manifest, it commences from the potential form, which is the state when the reality is formed and solidified in the heart or mind. There are few highlights we need to know about turning potentiality to reality.

First, according to Pastor Joel Osteen of Lakewood Church, "Victors are men who talk themselves into victory before actually achieving it". The scripture in the book of James describes the tongue of every man as a small helm that turns a great ship. Learning the effective use of words can contribute greatly to the extent of success and achievement a man record in his lifetime. Joel further stressed the right use of words when he said "When you speak to yourself the right way, courage comes, determination comes, and vision comes."

> **Words are powerful tools a man must learn to use rightly**

Further into the metamorphosis of potentiality into reality is using your skills set well and learning new ones. With the necessary and adequate skills set, you put yourself at an advantage to make good use of every idea. You are the best architect of your thoughts. Sharing your thoughts with others has its advantages but when your skills set doesn't contribute significantly to your idea or goals, the probability of success is fairly low. More so, you can employ the right set of skills when you know it's not among your skills set.

> **Skills and abilities are tools that release a man's potentials.**

In your Journey to becoming a champion, you need God every step of the way. Because ultimately when all fails, it is only God that can be your source of hope and strength. Also, as I have explained in previous chapters, for every step you take in life and in your ambition to become a champion, you need God's foresight. However, for God to be involved in your pursuit, there are certain things you should not do. That's why in the Bible, whenever God gave promises to those he loves, he always started by saying "If you obey my commandments" that is to say, the promises are dependent on your obedience. So, below is an outline of 5 important key points on involving God as your helper.

For championship, you need God every step of the way

- Never be an offender
- Never give the devil a chance
- Your salvation must be intact
- Never let self-overrule your calling
- Put god first and commit your ways to his care

As earlier said, everyone born of Christ carried in him/her the seed of a champion. But when a fertile land isn't cultivated, you cannot know the extent of produce it can give, likewise, when you don't give necessary and adequate attention to the sleeping champion in you, the exploits, the new things, the tremendous and awesome wonders that God wants to wrought on earth through you will not be realized.

Turning your potential to reality requires a lot of sacrifice. Let's consider 7 people who made huge sacrifices, passed all God's tests and emerged champions by following 7 vitals rules that will help bring out the championship in you.

- Trust in God (Abraham)
- Be patient (Joseph)
- Fight for the truth no matter what (Moses)
- Look beyond the now, to the future (Ruth)
- Be courageous in face of difficulty (David)
- Be persistent (Elisha)
- Follow peace with all men (Nelson Mandela)

Trust in God: The Example of Abraham: A champion always learns to trust in God, and if you want to be a champion you must also learn to trust in God. Putting your trust in God is like small kids allowing his/her parents to take care of them. Because God is Omnipotent, God is Omnipresence and God is Omnipotent, he knows all and sees all. He know if that choice will not favor you eventually; he knows if there is a trap waiting for you; he knows if that business plan will fail, even though the plan looks flawless; he knows if that partner will betray you, even though to you he/she seems so perfect; he knows the end from the beginning so you should at all times learn to put your trust in him.

If God says stops, and all your guts is telling you to go, what will you do☐Let's take a lesson from Abraham, in Genesis 12:1 "The LORD had said to Abram, "Go from your country, your people and your father's household to the land I will show you." God here told Abraham to abandon all he has worked for, all his relationships, his people, family, business, country and everything he has come to love and go to a strange place he knew nothing about. Tell me about Irrational and illogical decisions and I'll show you the decision

Abraham took which was to trust in God. I mean, who does that? Leave everything for nothing? Well, Abraham did and it worked out for him for good. The question is why? Abraham trusted in God, Abraham understood that God could see the future and God must have known that his future is not there in his father's god; Abraham believed in God's greater judgment and discernment. Any person that follows Abraham's model is sure to be a champion, because nothing pays better than putting your whole trust in the Lord.

Be Patient: The Joseph example: patience is a virtue not many are opportuned to have, that's why when Paul wrote on the fruits of the spirit in Galatians 5:22 he emphasized "But the fruit of the Spirit is love, joy, peace, patience, kindness, goodness, faithfulness". Patience here is one of the fruits that a believer bears as a result of having the Holy Spirit within them. God values patience in every believer and at the same time God demands it.

God's plan for you to be a champion includes you having the virtue of patience, if you do not already have it. God is going to take you through a series of trials and ordeals that will be testing your patience; events and scenarios that are meant to train you to become exceptionally patient as God will want. Joseph in his lifetime displayed an uncanny kind of patience that always thrilled and at the same time surprised me. His Patience started from when he was sold into slavery by his jealous brothers, to when Potiphar's wife framed him for attempted rape, and to when he was forgotten in prison. Joseph displayed patience and never wavered in his faith in God, he always trusted in God and kept on, until eventually his patience paid off and he became the governor of Egypt; that is from being a slave in prison to being a governor in the palace married to royalty. God totally transformed his life. The account of this can be found in the book of Genesis chapters 39-45.

Fight for the Truth no matter what: The example of Moses. Sometimes defending the truth comes at a difficult cost, but that might just be your ultimate test. For people like Abraham Lincoln, there was no price he was not willing to pay to see an end to the evil of slavery and for Nelson Mandela, who after spending 23 years in prison was offered freedom in February 1985, he refused freedom, not at the cost of the continued oppression of the apartheid regime. The courageous character of fighting for justice comes within the territory of champion hood; most champions, like we see above, became true champions when they decided to fight and die for what is right. The first act Moses did that expressed his desire to see the people of Israel free from slavery resulted in a Murder when "he went to see his own people and watched them suffering under forced labor. He saw a Hebrew, one of his own people, being beaten by an Egyptian. He looked all around, and when he didn't see anyone, he beat the Egyptian to death and hid the body in the sand (Exodus 2:11). The action, though not sanctioned by God, directed Moses to the path that would eventually see God call him. No matter where you find yourself, and no matter the condition you are in, never turn your back on the truth and doing what is right, because by doing what is right and helping others, you are actually doing the will of God as he said:

> "For I was hungry and you gave me something to eat, I was thirsty and you gave me something to drink, I was a stranger and you invited me in, I needed clothes and you clothed me, I was sick and you looked after me, I was in prison and you came to visit me" — *Matthew 25:35.*

What Jesus meant here was that,

> "Whatever you did for one of the least of these brothers and sisters of mine, you did for me"
> - *Matthew 25:40b*

Look beyond the now, to the future: The example of Ruth: the world is filled with many get- rich quick schemes, flashy misleading opportunities that promise fortunes, illegal activities promising riches of all kinds, things all contrary to the will and commandments of God. The thing about these flashy luxury and opportunities is that there's always someone saying try this, and take this risk and you get what you are looking for. But the question is are you willing to stake your future and eternity on something so temporal and false God's champions always look beyond the now, and God expects you to look beyond now. The life of Ruth teaches more than enough lessons in this aspect because even though she had suffered so much loss and setbacks with her mother-in-law, she looked beyond the current challenges into the possibilities of what the God of Naomi can do; so she vowed loyalty saying,

> **"Don't urge me to leave you or to turn back from you. Where you go I will go, and where you stay I will stay. Your people will be my people and your God my God"**
> *- Ruth 1:16.*

This decision was the life changer for Ruth, she eventually got a wonderful young man named Boaz as husband, and their son, Obed was the grandfather of King David; and from their lineage came our Lord Jesus Christ. Always look beyond the now, and look to the future possibilities God promised you, trust in his word, that he wants to make you successful, victorious and triumphant in all you do.

Be courageous in the face of difficulty: The Example of David: Having faith and trusting in God alone most times does not take the problem away. It was for this same reason the Bible says that,

> **"Thus also faith by itself, if it does not have works, is dead "** *- James 2:17.*

You can have all the faith in the world and trust in God 100 percent, those two alone may not be able to solve the equation, you still need to put some action to it. God's plan for you to be a champion includes you getting up and taking control of your life, and putting your faith and trust in God to the test. David was just a shepherd boy when he was anointed King of Israel. Yes, David trusted in God, Yes, David had faith, but if that was all David had, his anointing would have started and ended in the desert as a shepherd.

David had to take courageous action that put his anointing, faith and trust in God to the test. When David heard of how the giant, Goliath, made mockery of the armies of Israel and the name of the living God, he could not stand it; he had to do something, and that meant being courageous against a physically superior foe. From the King himself to the least soldier in the field, they all tried to convince David to stay off the fight with Goliath, but no, David knew this was his chance to make the name of the Lord great, he knew it was time to put his anointing to the test, and that he did. David's military exploits and victories meant he was not just courageous in one thing; he was courageous in many things, even in times when his spirit seemed to be broken. On a particular occasion,

> **"David was greatly distressed because the men were talking of stoning him; each one was bitter in spirit because of his sons and daughters"-** *1 Samuel 30:6.*

If it were you what would you have done☐Would you have blamed God☐Or your enemies or maybe found someone else to take the blame, or will you simply run away☐What would you do when you seem to have lost everything and at the same time your own people are ready to kill because their city had been "destroyed by fire and their wives and sons and daughters taken captive (1 Samuel 30:3b)." But David "found strength in the Lord his God". (1 Samuel 30:6b). His show of courage here was monumental as "David said to Abiathar the priest, the son of Ahimelek, "Bring me the ephod." Abiathar brought it to him, and David inquired of the Lord, "Shall I pursue this raiding party? Will I overtake them? "Pursue them," he answered. "You will certainly overtake them and succeed in the rescue (1 Samuel 30:7,8)" It was still because of David's unflinching courage that he could withstand more than a decade that King Saul chased him and wanted to kill him. David's exemplary show of courage is a model to every champion and champion-to-be; because without courage like that of David, there is no sit for you in the place for champions.

Be Persistent: The Example of Elisha: Have you ever asked, how many times do you have to try before you give up? Some may say until when you are tired, some say try a couple of times, and if it keeps failing then it is not going to work ever. But how many times does God expects us to try? Let us see a parable by Jesus,

> "Suppose you went to a friend's house at midnight, wanting to borrow three loaves of bread. You say to him, 'A friend of mine has just arrived for a visit, and I have nothing for him to eat.' And suppose he calls out from his bedroom, 'Don't bother me. The door is locked for the night, and my family and I are all in bed. I can't help you.' But I tell you this—though he won't do it for friendship's sake, if you keep knocking long enough, he will get up and give you whatever you need because of your shameless persistence" - *Luke 11:5-8.*

Note the word there "shameless persistence". It is an attitude Jesus was trying to emphasize for us to have whenever we are asking anything from God. Shameless persistence is the kind of persistence that even you know is becoming embarrassing; you do this only when you know the importance of what it is you are asking for. Long before Jesus told this parable, someone displayed this kind of shameless persistence and almost became like a stalker because he wanted something and he was willing to cover his shame for what he wanted. That man was Elisha, and because he was shamelessly persistent he got a double portion of Elijah's power. At first, "Elijah said to Elisha, "Stay here; the Lord has sent me to Bethel." But Elisha said, "As surely as the Lord lives and as you live, I will not leave you" (2 Kings 2:2).

Then again he said to him, "Stay here, Elisha; the Lord has sent me to Jericho." And he replied, "As surely as the Lord lives and as you live, I will not leave you." So they went to Jericho." And for the third time "Elijah said to him, "Stay here; the Lord has sent me to the Jordan. And he replied, "As surely as the Lord lives and as you live, I will not leave you." So the two of them walked on." And when he saw that this shamelessly persistent fellow wasn't going anywhere, he asked, "Tell me, what can I do for you before I am taken from you?" You know, left to Elijah alone, he wouldn't have asked Elisha this question, he would have been taken away, had it been Elisha left him for a second. Whatever you are doing, whatever you are trying to do or achieve, continue to be persistent and keep trying and trying until you finally hit your target.

Follow Peace with all Men: The Nelson Mandela example: Nelson Mandela's struggle to put an end to the apartheid regime cost him a lot, and most importantly it cost him his freedom for 27 years. But the 27 years he spent in the lonely prison on Robben Island was a pathway that led Mandela to greatness and eventually earned him his place as a champion. Mandela lost a lot of things while in prison, including his first wife, and even while in prison he was placed in solitary confinement, but all these never changed who he was at his core, it never made him violent or seek after revenge or personal gains; rather all he went through prepared him for the future of making South Africa a united nation and the strongest economy in Africa during his time. By remaining true to his purpose, his call during his time of trial, Nelson Mandela passed God's ultimate test for him. That's why when he eventually became president of South Africa, he pursued peace from all angles; he tried as much as possible to balance all the races and act according to God's word to "follow peace with all men".

This was the same model our Lord Jesus, and his disciples followed all through the trials and persecution they experienced. They never took the violent part or the part of revenge, understanding that this never really solves the problem. God's plan for you to be a champion includes living in peace with everyone. And it is in this direction that the Bible says,

> **"If it is possible, as far as it depends on you, live at peace with everyone"** - *Romans 12:18*

Rev. Martin Luther King Jr. had every reason to be violent, as the rights of blacks were openly violated and they were segregated, but no matter how much the government, police and people pushed him, he never flayed from his purpose and God's direction which is that of peace. No matter what the world throws at you, no matter the persecution or trials you may be going through, always learn to be at peace with everyone, because true champions never, ever achieved victory through violence, unless when it is beyond their power to control.

25 ATTITUDES TO BECOME A CHAMPION
Have
1. A vision - visualise yourself as a champion and dream it
2. Determine to be a champion
3. Set a clear goals - Aim high
4. Break down your goals to objectives
5. Have passion and pursue your passion
6. Believe in yourself with all tenacity
7. Confront your fears
8. Be willing to pay the price
9. Go beyond your comfort zone
10. Leave a live of purpose
11. Tackle your weakness and boost your strength
12. Discipline yourself
13. Be optimistic to win - be positive
14. Learn from mentors/coach/role models
15. Acquire skills, practice and train
16. Be acquitted with necessary rules, principles and guidelines

17. Master your skills
18. Be hard working and make sacrifices
19. Don't procrastinate
20. Leave a live of purpose
21. Be consistent and persistent
22. Don't quiet
23. Count your failure as stepping
24. Always have the heart of champion

Esther

Esther was born at a time when Israel was in captivity as a consequence of their disobedience to God. When Esther's parents were killed, her cousin Mordecai adopted her as his daughter. Not only was Esther an ordinary woman living in a foreign land, but she was part of a minority race held in low esteem, such that when she later became the queen, Mordecai advised her to keep secret her Jewish nationality. God chose Esther to do through her what He had planned before she was even born. He works sovereignly in the lives of ordinary people who submit to His ways. She was one of many Jewish children whose parents died but rather than becoming rebellious and resentful over her troubled life, Esther was obedient to Mordecai, who brought her up.

When Esther was taken for the King's beauty contest, she had no choice in the matter. Whether or not the King chose her as his wife, she would become his property—never allowed to return to her life with Mordecai, yet she trusted God. She did not become proud because of her beauty. Her humble spirit shined brightly and she won favor in the eyes of all who saw her, including Hegai the king's eunuch who had been put in charge of the virgins. When the king summoned a virgin, the virgin was allowed to bring in with her whatever she thought would make her most attractive to the king. However, when Esther was summoned, she took with her nothing except what Hegai advised—resulting in a positive response from the king. When Esther spent the night with the king, God caused his heart to *"love Esther more than all the women, and she won grace and favor in his sight"* (Esther 2:17).

When Mordecai learned of a plot to annihilate the Jews, he asked Esther to implore the king to step in. When out of fear she declined, Mordecai helped her realize the reason God chose her to be queen. He said, *"If you keep silent at this time, relief and deliverance will rise for the Jews from another place, but you and your father's house will perish. And who knows whether you have not come to the kingdom for such a time as this"* (Esther 4:14). With this reminder, Esther braced up. She realized that her rise to royalty had nothing to do with her beauty or God granting her a comfortable life. Instinctively Esther knew to turn to God for her strength. Rather than jumping into action, Esther spent time in prayer, fasting, and waiting for God to direct how and when to approach the king (Esther 4:15-16). She declared, "If I die I die". Her love for God and for her people took precedence over her love for her own life. Through Esther's resolve to trust in God, she influenced the king and saved her people and her courage was celebrated by a feast of Purim and a decree went out from that day on, *"these days of Purim should be remembered and kept throughout every generation"* (Esther 9:28).

Source: Adapted from the Bible- Esther Chapters 2, 4 and 9

> **The difference between mediocre and champion is usually a very small extra effort**

2 Timothy 2:15 - *Do your best to present yourself to God as one approved, a worker who does not need to be ashamed and who correctly handles the word of truth*

9

THE CORE OF EVERY CHAMPION

Great things are accomplished with passion

Chapter 9
THE CORE OF EVERY CHAMPION

*The Lord makes firm the steps of the one who delights in him;
though he may stumble, he will not fall, for the Lord upholds
him with his hand. Psalm 37:23-24*

What is a Core: A core is your center point; a core is a place from which all the energy in your body gets inspired. If your core is blue, then everything that flows out of you will be blue. A core, in this context, is the ground, soil, or place from which everything in your life grows. Your every decision is influenced by your core, your every dream is affected by your core, your hopes, aspirations, targets, and goals are all influenced by the kind of core that sits at your center. A core can be an ideology or a standard principle that guides your life; a core might be something your society or family or peers have helped to shape you into, that ultimately determines every decision or action you take. In this book, I have divided the cores into eight major parts, one of which is yours, because whether consciously or unconsciously you have a core that influences all you do. While some people are vividly aware of what their core is, some are not. However, here is a list of cores that guide the majority of us;

- Family-centered core
- Money centered core
- Business-centered core
- Work centered core
- Pleasure-centered core
- Power centered core
- Religious centered core
- God-centered core

Family-Centered Core: Here, the focus is always the family; whatever that person does the family is still involved, whether immediate or extended family. If he has a business, the family comes first in that business, if it is work, he subjugates work for his family, and his/her priorities are always centered on family.

Money Centered Core: Money, irrespective of how it comes, is the focus here. A person with a money-centered core has no moral limits and can do anything for money because the need to make the next bucks is what is always on their mind. This core places money and material things above human life or moral standards, so they have no ethical backgrounds and do things as long as it brings more money.

Business Centered Core: The difference between a money-centered core and a business centered core is that a business centered core is particularly interested in business ventures or his own business; he is focused on moving his business to the next level, on being the top earner in the market, of standing above all other businesses in his league. A business centered person forgets family, God, religion, and places his primary focus on his business.

Work-Centered Core: A work centered core does everything from the lens of work. He is working at home in the morning, on his way to work he is on the phone working or reading the next report, he closes late and takes work home. Even during family time, a work centered core will make an excuse from his family to fulfill his work obligation. A work centered person works even on Sundays when they are supposed to be in the presence of God. All they think is work, the next promotion, the next bonus and how to be the best of the best and impress the boss.

Pleasure-centered core: A pleasure centered core, is always focused on pleasure: what to drink, what to eat, the next party, the next show, the best dancing steps, the latest attires, the latest shows, the most relaxed party. A pleasure centered core subjugates all other things, including personal health and safety, so that they can have fun and be crowned social kings or queens. Whatever a pleasure-centered person does, they do so that they can up their stats in the social circle. Even when a pleasure-centered person goes to church or for any religious activity, it is always done because they want to achieve a social or pleasure driven goal.

Power Centered Core: A Power Centered Core is always thinking about power in whatever form it presents itself. Whether political power, spiritual power, social power through fame, they are always power conscious and power mongers. All they do, all they say is because they want power or are seeking to gain it. A power centered core will do anything to gain power. Even in the church there are people with power centered core posing as pastors or ministers of God, but over time you discover they cannot hide their nature and it becomes very obvious that what thrills them is a need to control people and be powerful; and not a necessity to serve God or preserve his kingdom.

Religious Centered Core: A religious centered core is almost like a fanatic, because they are enthusiastic about anything religious, and take it very personally. A religious centered core is always in the church day and night, always involved in one church activity or the other. They are always the forerunners in anything involving the church. They always have suggestions, are always volunteering, and they do all these to the detriment of their family life, work life, and personal life. And the uniqueness of a religious centered core is that it is not God-centered.

God-Centered Core: A God-centered core is from the school of thought that says "Seek ye first the Kingdom of God and all other things shall be added unto you." A God-centered core seeks to promote the glory of God in anything they do; whether at home, at work, in their businesses or in their social lives, God is always at the center. If they are business owners, when you read their vision and mission statement, you see God in the center of it. In their homes, you can see and experience the influence of God in every life; at work and in the office, their benevolent and God inspired nature makes everybody love them, and they always excel.

The long and short of it is that a God-centered core is a core every aspiring champion or person should have. The reason is not far-fetched, whether you have a family, business, work, power, pleasure, or religious centered core, you always give too much attention to one thing, and that is bad. But, when you are God-centered, you learn through the Holy Spirit to balance everything righteously. In my life so far, I have read so many books, being to seminars and conferences, listened to tapes from great authors, but all these knowledge combined are not up to the knowledge you get from reading the Bible.

First, the Bible teaches you to seek God; that's the first lesson and instruction. It tells you to obey all of his commandments, to love him and not serve any other God. Then what next☐The Bible then tells you to love everyone, the way you love yourself. In this context, the Bible defines love thus;

"Love is patient; love is kind. It does not envy, and it does not boast, it is not proud. It does not dishonor others. It is not self-seeking; it is not easily angered; it keeps no record of wrongs. Love does not delight in evil but rejoices with the truth. It always protects, always trusts, always hope, always perseveres. Love never fails. But where there are prophecies, they will cease; where there are tongues, they will be stilled; where there is knowledge, it will pass away"- 1 Corinthians 13:4.

Do you know what happens when you love this way? You automatically become a hero, a champion to everyone, because it takes loving like this to have a heart as Jesus did, to preach like Paul the Apostle did, to fight like David fought, to be patient like Joseph was, and to trust like Abraham trusted. To be loyal like Ruth was loyal, to be peaceful and forgiving like Nelson Mandela was, to be calm and courageous in the face of violence, like Rev. Martin Luther King Jr. was, to be caring and loving like Mother Theresa was, to shun evil as Abraham Lincoln did. To be a true champion, you must have a God-centered core that obeys all of God's instructions and balances all aspects of his/her life based on God's words.

Nelson Mandela

Rolihlahla Mandela was born into the Madiba clan in the village of Mvezo, in the Eastern Cape, on 18 July 1918. In 1930, when he was 12 years old, his father died and the young Rolihlahla became a ward of Jongintaba at the Great Place in Mqhekezweni. Hearing the stories about his ancestors' valor during the wars of resistance, he dreamed also of making his own contribution to the freedom struggle of his people. He attended primary school in Qunu, where his teacher, Miss Mdingane, gave him the name Nelson, in accordance with the custom of giving all schoolchildren "Christian" names.

After several attempts at studying, Nelson eventually completed his BA through the University of South Africa, went back to Fort Hare for his graduation in 1943, and in 1989, while in the last months of his imprisonment, he obtained an LLB through the University of South Africa. A two-year diploma in law on top of his BA allowed Mandela to practise law, and in August 1952 he and Oliver Tambo established South Africa's first black law firm, Mandela & Tambo. At the end of 1952 he was banned for the first time. As a restricted person he was only permitted to watch in secret as the Freedom Charter was adopted in Kliptown on 26 June 1955.

Mandela was arrested in a countrywide police swoop on 5 December 1956, which led to the 1956 Treason Trial. Men and women of all races found themselves in the dock in the marathon trial that only ended when the last 28 accused, including Mandela, were acquitted on 29 March 1961.

While facing a death penalty, his words to the court at the end of his famous "Speech from the Dock" on 20 April 1964 became immortalised:

"I have fought against white domination, and I have fought against black domination. I have cherished the ideal of a democratic and free society in which all persons live together in harmony and with equal opportunities. It is an ideal which I hope to live for and to achieve. But if needs be, it is an ideal for which I am prepared to die." (Speech from the Dock quote by Nelson Mandela on 20 April 1964)

In spite of all odds: death penalty, several arrests and imprisonments, on 10 May 1994 he was inaugurated as South Africa's first democratically elected President, and on retirement continued to work with the Nelson Mandela Children's Fund he set up in 1995 and established the Nelson Mandela Foundation and The Mandela Rhodes Foundation.

Source: Adapted from
https://www.nelsonmandela.org/content/page/biography

> **Discover why you are born and achieve it before you die**

Ephesians 2;10- *For we are God's handwork, created in Christ Jesus to do good works, which God prepared in advance for us to do.*

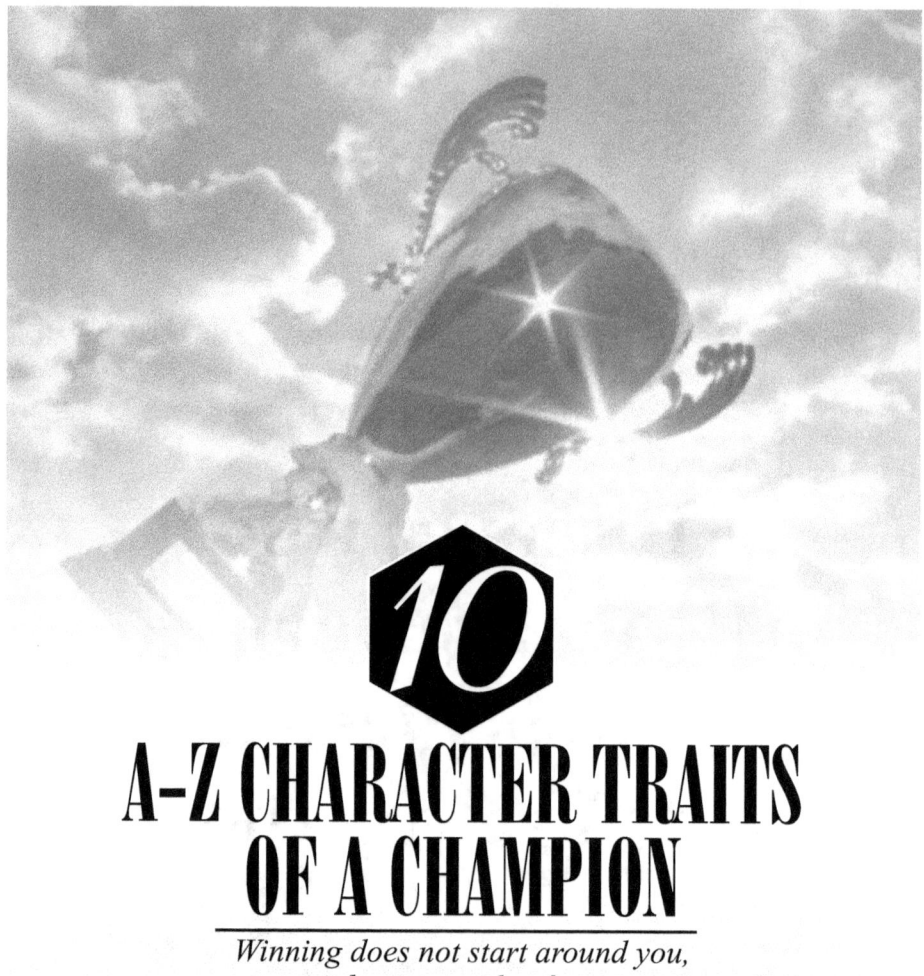

10

A–Z CHARACTER TRAITS OF A CHAMPION

*Winning does not start around you,
it begins inside of you*

Chapter 10
A-Z CHARACTER TRAITS OF A CHAMPION

Whatever you do, work at it with all your heart, as working for the Lord, not for human masters, 24 since you know that you will receive an inheritance from the Lord as a reward. It is the Lord Christ you are serving - Colossians 3:23-24.

Here you will find 24 values that make up the character traits every champion should have; as you read them, work towards developing them in your life and you will see your paradigm shift for the better.

- A- Altruism:
- B- Benevolence
- C- Commitment
- D- Diligence
- E- Ethical
- F- Faith
- G- Genuineness (originality)
- H- Humility

A-Z Character Traits of A Champion

I- Innovative
J- Just
K- Knowledgeable
L- Love
M- Modest, not flamboyant
N- Non-conforming, steadfast
O- Obedience
P- Patience
Q- Quality
R- Resilience
S- Self-control
T- Transparency
U- Unity
V- Valor
W- Wisdom
X- Xoxo, show some love
Y- Yes, Can-do attitude
Z- Zealousness

TIPS TO BECOME A CHAMPION

Here I have outlined 14 powerful tips that will help you become a champion:

1. **Connect with God and Find your purpose:** Through Prayer and meditation, you petition God to give you direction on what your purpose is in life. Find a quiet place to seek God's face, get all the concentration and time you need, by doing this you give God a chance to actually whisper something to you. Receive the life of champion by giving yourself wholly to God,

2. **Always in His presence:** Feed the champion in you by constantly fellowship with God via Bible study and prayer

3. **Discover what (or who) you need to make it work:** Once you identify your purpose or calling, your next step will be to discover and write out what or who you need to fulfill that purpose. If it's a person, you might want to have a conversation with them, and if it's a thing you work towards getting it ready for your journey.

4. **Master your God Given Skills for your Purpose:** Before God gives you a purpose or calling, he gives you something within to fulfill that purpose. That's your skill or talent. You should learn to harness and master your skill or talent. Train yourself every day in it and be better than the previous day.

5. **Find a Mentor:** Yes, even as a believer you need a mentor. They can be from the church, your office, but it has to be someone you trust, can confide in, and someone that is passionate about what you are trying to achieve.

6. **Learn:** read and study wide about your purpose: Explore ideas, studies and all things that you know are relevant to your purpose and calling. No knowledge is ever wasted, so never stop learning

7. **Have a strict disciplined routine:** After setting your short term and long term goals, discipline yourself to always keep them and stay honorable to all you have set out to do.

8. **Stay positive:** You may win some and lose some, you will get encouragement and you will be discouraged, but at all times always stay positive and have faith in your purpose.

9. **Surround yourself with people who are passionate about what you do:** There is no time to slack and look back, the work of God is all too important for that. So, whoever is a hindrance or setback in your journey, you'll need to get them out of the way and surround yourself with people who are optimistic about what you do.

10. **Have standard for excellence:** A champion always has a standard, that is unique and special and that's a standard of excellence everyone will come to admire. In your pursuit you will have to create a unique standard of excellence that others will come to connect you with.

11. **Trust in God always**: In all you do always put your trust in God because he is the "author and finisher of our faith".

12. **Be obedient to God always:** Follows God lead. Heed to every instruction from God to you. Be led by the spirit of God always

13. **Love God:** Love God and love Him more every of your life day – 1 Cor 2:9

14. **Live a discipline and principled life**: Set yourself apart from every life distractions and defilement

Mark Zuckerberg

Mark Zuckerberg was born on May 14, 1984, in White Plains, New York into a comfortable, well-educated family; his father, Edward Zuckerberg, ran a dental practice attached to the family's home while his mother, Karen, worked as a psychiatrist. This advantageous background notwithstanding, Mark worked hard to achieve his own dream. This great achiever, from his college dorm room, co-founded the popular social-networking website, Facebook. Mark left Harvard after his sophomore year to concentrate on the site. Since then, the user base has grown to more than 2 billion people, which makes Zuckerberg a multi billionaire. His interest in computers was from an early age of about 12, when he used Atari BASIC to create a messaging program that he named "Zucknet." His father used the program in his dental office, so that the receptionist could inform him of a new patient without yelling across the room. Zucknet was also used by the family to communicate within the house.

Mark Zuckerberg later studied at Phillips Exeter Academy, an exclusive preparatory school in New Hampshire, where he showed talent in fencing, and became the captain of the school's team. He also excelled in literature, earning a diploma in classics. He, however, remained fascinated by computers, and continued to work on developing new programs. He remained focused, not losing his dream, in spite of other side achievements. Hence, when he was still in high school, he created an early version of the music software Pandora, which he called Synapse. His other feats include CourseMatch, which helped students choose their classes based on the course selections of other users, and Facemash. This champion continued steadfastly, improving his efforts till, with his friends, he created the site that allowed users to create their own profiles, upload photos, and communicate with other users. The group ran the site—first called The Facebook—out of a dorm room at Harvard until June 2004.

Since amassing his sizeable fortune, Zuckerberg has used his millions to fund a variety of philanthropic causes. He is not self-centered, he is altruistic, benevolent, committed to his dream and very diligent, all traits for championship.

Source: Adapted from
https://www.biography.com/business-figure/mark-zuckerberg

11

INVOLVING GOD TO BE A CHAMPION

You have the greatest treasure in you when you have Jesus

Chapter 11

INVOLVING GOD TO BE A CHAMPION

in all your ways submit to him, and he will make your paths straight - Prov. 3:6

In your Journey to becoming a champion, you need God in every step of the way. Because ultimately when all fails, it is only God that can be your source of hope and strength. Also, as I have explained in previous chapters, every step you take in life and in your ambition to become a champion you need God's foresight, as even the wisest of the wise affirmed this. However, God does not readily involve himself with everyone, for God to be involved in your pursuit there are certain things you must never not do. That's why in the bible whenever God gave promises to those he loved he always started by saying "If you obey my commandments" that is to say, the promises are contingent on your obedience. So therefore I have outlined 5 important key points you must always keep at the back of your mind in your goal of involving God as your helper. These five points are a summary of the numerous laws of God, however if you manage to abide by them, then God will not be far from you.

1. **Never be an Offender:** Do not let sin into your life for whatever reason, acquaint yourself with those things God does not like and stay away from them- Proverb 28:13. The bible says God hates "a lying tongue" then you try as much as possible that your tongue never tells a lie. The bible says God hates "pride" then you always allow yourself to be humble. Never be an offender means never be caught in a position where your conscience questions you. Remember Samson.

2. **Never Give the Devil a Chance:** The devil is sneaky and manipulative, always be on the lookout for his tricks- 1 Peter 5:8. We have examined previously how he tricked David into taken a census against God's will, well the thing is, if he tricked David he can trick you too. Through prayer and constant connection with God, we become aware of the schemes of Satan and ultimately avoid them.

3. **Your Salvation must be intact:** (Hebrew 6:4-6) Like I mentioned before, the fulfillment of God's promises in your life is contingent on your obedience of all his commands. This ensures your salvation. As a believer you must search yourself at all times to make sure, you are still on the right track with God, to ensure you have not strayed from the faith. Because the moment the joy of your salvation begins to drain, then your power and hope to succeed begins to drain too.

4. **Never let self-overrule your calling:** We all have desires, desires that spring from your physical impulses. These desires sometimes compete with God calling and purpose in your life. That should never happen, your desire and fleshly impulses must always be put under control, and never should you subjugate your calling because you want to indulge in whatever your body desires.

5. **Put God first and Commit your ways to his care**: (Matthew 6:33) Whatever you do or intend to do, learn to always put God first, consult and inform him of your actions. A lot of good comes out of these, because God tells you if this is okay or not and at the

same time he gives you direction you couldn't otherwise have gotten. By putting God first and committing your works into God's hand it shows your reverence for him, and whoever reverences God, God always reverences that person.

AWAKEN THE CHAMPION IN YOU
As earlier said, everyone born of Christ carried in him/her the seed of a champion. But when a fertile land isn't cultivated, you cannot know the extent of produce it can give, likewise, when you don't given necessary and adequate attention to the sleeping champion in you, the exploits, the new things, the tremendous and awesome wonders that God want to wrought on earth through you might be lived out. Below are areas of life that require a keen attention and cultivation if truly you desire to live out the champion in you. THE WORLD IS WAITING FOR YOU

The world is still in dire need of innovation and improvement. The society has never been any much in need than now. You are a child of God and it is in you to make God known everywhere you go. You have the gift to say soothing words to the dying world. You could be the symbol of hope in the midst of weakness and pains around. You could be the voice for the voiceless. You know what you can achieve. It is in you. Do not hesitate, because Jesus never hesitated. For some three years and at a very youthful age, Jesus Christ did very well. Had Jesus decided to keep quiet in the face of the errors the Pharisees were committing, things would still have been very difficult for the followers. Just think about it. The people would have been going to the synagogue only to be handed down laws too strict yet not helping.

Had David not risen to the occasion, nothing would have happened. He became a champion of the age. Moses would never have been known had he not risked it and saved a race. Whether he agreed to take risk or not he will still die. He might not die or pay any price for not taking risk, but death is for all mortals; he would still die one day. Joseph was in the house of pleasure and fame. Had he slept with Potiphar's wife, he would have earthly pleasure but that would never save his soul or have a place for his people's interest.

When the days drew near for the word of the Lord to spread, the Apostles risked their lives and today we have the message of Christ which is our salvation. Mary Magdalene knew what she wanted. She was of the mind to hold on to the greatest gift which was being saved from the life of sin. She held on to the one who could save her, even in the face of being taunted. She knew that Jesus was what she needed and she never let that opportunity to go by.

Nehemiah was an able administrator. He knew that the house of the Lord would be rebuilt. He did it with zeal and hope. His name has gone down to be among those faithful to the cause of the Lord. Daniel, Jerimiah, Hosea, Nehemiah, Jacob etc. They were all champions.

You have the grit of a champion. If you have music as your part to help bring the Lord closer to the world, you should do. If you have coordinating and leading as your key role, then do it. If it is singing, do it to the best of your ability. Always remember that whatever you do should be done with happiness and comportment such that people would derive joy from it and give praise to God. The world is incomplete without you. There is enough vacuum because you have not contributed your quota.

YOU HAVE WHAT IT TAKES TO BE A CHAMPION
You are a child of God and with God all things are possible. You have the power of prayer to conquer at the spiritual level. You have been initiated into the kingdom of God. His power is above every other power (cf Judges 14:5). Sometimes, you could be tired and weak. There could be problems you are left to face alone. But having the power of the Most High is the greatest. It is the most important. In times like that, get to Him who made all things possible in prayer and you will survive. God will not forsake His children. He will always guide and lead them. You have God like David had such that he firmly faced Goliath without losing any hope.

Abraham was very much firm in his believes in God. You should always live by praying because every other thing will be in place. Physical training and improvement should equally apply to you. Being a champion does not end with just living with the achievements you have made. There should always be an avenue for improvement. The quest for improvement is in us humans, but champions do it much better.

Always push it harder because the world has no joy when efforts are not put into it. The beautiful things are those things that came from hard work and consistent practice. Gold is never found in its raw state. It is a product of long search and persistent refinement until it attains the alluring nature it has. Gold remains to this day a most precious element. Even the Queen of Sheba was effusive with words of praise when she saw how much gold had been used to beautify the palace of King Solomon.

Had champions of history not taken time to search deeply into the earth after a weakening work against the rubbish around. Remember that in every competition, only one winner emerges. Therefore be very much prepared (1 Cor. 9:24). And for the heavenly race you are not a champion until the very last (2 Timothy 4:7).

JESUS CHRIST OUR GREAT CHAMPION
Jesus is the greatest champion, and he should be the role model of all champions. Jesus is a physical champion and he is a spiritual champion and even till this very moment he is still a champion. He is winning battles upon battles every day. Jesus is the only champion who never lost a battle, and won the war. That's why to you and me we should always look up to Jesus as model in our quest to become champions. Because Jesus was a flawless champion, so which better champion can you learn from☐From birth till death the life of Jesus is a lesson, and within it there is a lesson to be learnt. Therefore, in your journey to becoming a champion, read his words, read his works, seeks his face and trust in that powerful name and indeed all your hope and desires will be fulfilled.

The coming of Jesus into this world is not an historical fact but it was actually a reality as He came to champion a cause for God's elect and the fallen men. The fallen nature of man left us all in a despicable state such that we couldn't really see God for what He is and who we are in Him nor find it easy following all the laws He gave, once a man breaks any of the law, he has broken all. The law couldn't make anything perfect, the law delivered by God was intended to be our schoolmaster, our guardian to see that in ourselves, our flesh is no good thing (Gal 3:24). Jesus, the word of God as named in the times that predates His coming was there with God from the very start and the only way to really deliver men from the oppression of Sin, death and Satan is that one mightier than this come and fight for the deliverance of man. The battle Jesus faced was severe but all through He was victorious. Man couldn't have been delivered if left to himself, but God in His infinite mercies came to save man by sending His son, Jesus.

Let us see briefly major ways whereby Jesus became our living and greatest champion:

☐ **Salvation from Sin:**
After man ate from the forbidden tree, the life of God in man died and the life of sin took dominion over man and afterwards, men could live before God as he ought and came under the slavery of Sin. God gave the law to help men aid in their walk back to God but many still fell under the deception of sin, and kept being under the slavery of sin. This wasn't the intention of God when He created man, hence God is left to arise for the salvation and deliverance of man. In the bid to accomplish this, God in the form of Man, came, humbled himself and was born in a lowly place like the manger, being the first son of Mary, the espoused wife of Joseph. The enemy of Man, Satan, knowing that God was intending to deliver man sent darts and fierce battle against the bay, the young and the adult Jesus, trying every means to bring Him down from fulfilling and winning the battle of man's deliverance. In all this, Jesus didn't lose gaze of the essence of His coming and kept pushing through till he took up the cross and was led up to Golgotha to die for the

sins of the whole world, hence paying the debts of sin for all men. And even for those that didn't believe in Him yet. To the glory of God, the battle could have been lost if the price of this world had come and find no hold on Jesus (John 14:30). Jesus showed man the way of the cross by being a champion in it. This act of Jesus carries the potentiality of delivering any man from the rule of sin for as many as can come to Him, belief in Him and confess with their mouth His lordship.

☐ **Salvation from Death:**

After the fall of man, death began to reign over man. At a point in time, God was so displeased with the way man continued to live his life and he decreed a reduction in the time to be spent here on earth by man (Gen 6:3) and decreed that His spirit will not contend with man any more. The state is a terrible one for man, as his days on earth is characterized by the fear of death (Heb 2:15). Rom 5:14 shows us that "Nevertheless, death reigned from the time of Adam to the time of Moses, even over those who did not sin by breaking a command, as did Adam, who is a pattern of one to come; vs 17a "For if, by the trespass of one man, death reigned through that one man…" This is a serious state where man has been left, but thanks to Jesus who championed the deliverance of man from death and it attending fear. Jesus came in the likeness of man to win the battle over death, and gave life to as many that comes to Him. John 10:10 "…I have come that they may have life and to have it to the full." Rom 5:18 further showed the results of Jesus' sacrifice "Consequently, just as one trespass resulted in the condemnation for all people, so also one righteous act resulted in justification and life for all people." The fear of death is done away with among those that come to Christ; they live life to the fullest.

☐ **Salvation from Satan's dominion:**

Since man fell, the Lordship and rulership of the earth was handed over to the devil as against God's plan. Jesus came leading all the way to fight for the deliverance of the earth from the dominion of Satan and handed over the authority on earth and in heaven to the ones who dearly follows him with full assurance of faith. The scripture says "Since the children have flesh and blood, He too shared in their humanity so that by His death He might break the power of Him who holds the power of death- that is, the devil- Heb 2:14"

Jesus championed many things for us as examples of our new nature in God and also among them is also destroying the dividing wall between us and God and hence reconciled us back (Eph 2:14). No man has ever done this and can ever do it. Jesus also, by His blood and flesh, He opened a new and living way into the heart of the Father, the Holies of Holies (Heb 10:19-20). So many more areas of life did Jesus wrought great things for every man on earth and finally was able to put the devil where he is, under our feet. Jesus became the only man to excel in all spheres of life without mincing words.

Larry Page

Lawrence 'Larry' Page is an American Computer Scientist and an internet entrepreneur who co-founded Google with Sergey Brin in 1998. Larry Page is the CEO of Google's parent company Alphabet Inc. Born on March 26, 1973, in East Lansing, Michigan, his father was a Ph. D in Computer Science and a professor at Michigan State University and his mother an instructor in computer programming. A voracious reader in his youth, Page spent a lot of time poring over Science & Technology books and magazines. Page always liked to invent things and at the age of 12 knew that someday he was going to start a company. Page holds a Bachelor of Science in Computer Engineering from the University of Michigan, with honors and a Master of Science in Computer Science from Stanford University.

Page took over as the CEO of Google in 2011 taking over the reins from Eric Schmidt and stepped down and handed over the charge to Sundar Pichai in 2015. Page is now the CEO of Alphabet and Sergey Brin its President.

Personal Life
In 2007, Larry Page married Lucinda Southworth, a research scientist and the sister of actress and model Carrie Southworth. Page and Southworth have two children born in 2009 and 2011.
Page's life has been hugely influenced by four factors; his grandfather's history in the early labor movement, his education in Montessori schools, his admiration for his hero- the visionary inventor Nikola Tesla, and his participation in the leadership institute at the University of Michigan's Engineering School. Page admitted in an interview that the hardships of his grandfather's story made him want to make Google an entirely different kind of workplace, one that, instead of crushing the dreams of workers, encouraged their pursuit.

Page suffers from paralyzed vocal cords that are caused by an autoimmune disease called Hashimoto's thyroiditis. The Page family foundation frequently donates to charities and in 2014 Page donated $15 million to aid the efforts against the Ebola virus epidemic in West Africa.

The 'Who Founded Google' Story
In the year 1995, while in the Stanford University, Larry Page and Sergei Brin initiated the process of developing a search engine as part of their research project & named it as the "BackRub". This search engine was designed to explore the connecting links between web pages so as to determine a site's authority.

In the year 1996, Page's web crawler began to explore the web, with Stanford home page serving as the initial phase. Later in the year 1998, Page and Brin decided to formally incorporate their company & set up their first data center in a garage.

Soon Page & Brin started looking for investors to back their initiative. Eventually, Andy Bechtolsheim, one of the founders of Sun Microsystems, invested about $100,000 in their company. Over a period of time, the duo managed to raise over $1 million.

Finally, Google, Inc. was established on September 7, 1998, with its first employee being Craig Silverstein, who later became Google's Director of Technology. Initially, Google served over 10,000 queries a day & steadily gained a reputation of the most reliable source of information. By 1999, it was serving over 500,000 queries a day and the company soon expanded from a mere four wall garage to now a mega office that is headquartered in Mountain View, California.

Achievements
In 2002, Page was named a World Economic Forum Global Leader for Tomorrow and along with Sergey Brin was named by MIT's Technology Review publication as one of the top 100

innovators in the world under the age of 35.

In 2004, Page and Brin received the Marconi Foundation's prize and were elected Fellows of the Marconi Foundation at Columbia University.

In 2004, X PRIZE chose Page as a trustee of their board and he was elected to the National Academy of Engineering. In 2005, Brin and Page were elected Fellows of the American Academy of Arts and Sciences.

In 2008 Page received the Communication Award from King Felipe at the Princess of Asturias Awards on behalf of Google.

In 2011, Page was ranked 24th on the Forbes list of billionaires, and as the 11th richest person in the U.S.

In 2009, Page received an honorary doctorate from the University of Michigan during a graduation commencement ceremony.

At the completion of 2014, Fortune magazine named Page its "Businessperson of the Year," declaring him "the world's most daring."

In October 2015, Page was named number one in Forbes' "America's Most Popular Chief Executives", as voted by its employees

Over the years, Google has achieved many spectacular milestones. Their audience continued to grow rapidly along with their reputation for being the most efficient, reliable firm offering relevant data search at maximum speeds.

Here are some of Google's accomplishments listed below.
Ad Sense, Google Maps, G-mail, Android, YouTube, Verizon Partnership, I-Phone Search

By partnering with Apple to provide the default search engine on iPhone's, Google gained a good foothold on the fast-growing mobile operating system. This led to a rapid growth & domination of Google in the mobile search market.

So, now you know the role that Larry Page and Google play in helping us complete our day-to-day assignments and do well in examinations.

Source: https://www.toppr.com/bytes/larry-page/

CONCLUSION

*You will only be remembered for the
impact you created in your lifetime*

CONCLUSION
For your new you to emerge, you have to think, plan and act like a champion

Jesus is the greatest champion, and he should be the role model of all champions. Jesus is both a physical and spiritual champion, and even till this very moment, he is still a champion. He is winning battles upon battles every day. Jesus is the only champion who never lost a battle and won the war. That's why to you and me, we should always look up to Jesus as a model in our quest to become champions. Because Jesus was a flawless champion, which better champion can you learn from From birth till death, the life of Jesus is a lesson. Therefore, in your journey to becoming a champion, read his words, read his works, seek his face, and trust in that powerful name, and indeed, all your hopes and desires will be fulfilled.

The coming of Jesus into this world is not a historical fact, but it was a reality as He came to champion a cause for God's elect and the fallen men. The fallen nature of man left us all in a despicable state such that we couldn't see God for what He is and who we are in Him; we do not find it easy following all the laws He gave because once a man breaks any of the law, he has broken all. The law couldn't make anything perfect, the law delivered by God was intended to be our schoolmaster, our guardian to see that in ourselves, and in our flesh is no good thing (Gal 3:24). Jesus, the word of God as named in the times that predates His coming was there with God from the very start, and the only way to deliver men from the oppression of sin, death, and Satan is that one mightier than these should come and fight for the deliverance of man. The battle Jesus faced was severe, but all through, He was victorious. Man couldn't have been delivered if left to himself, but God in His infinite mercies came to save man by sending His son, Jesus. Let us see briefly major ways whereby Jesus became our living and greatest champion:

Salvation from Sin:
After man ate from the forbidden tree, the life of God in man died, and the life of sin took dominion over man, and afterward, men came under the slavery of sin. God gave the law to help men in their walk back to God, but many still fell under the deception of sin and kept being under the slavery of sin. This wasn't the intention of God when He created man. Hence God in the form of a man came, humbled himself and was born in a lowly place like the manger, being the first son of Mary, the espoused wife of Joseph. The enemy of man, Satan, knowing that God intended to deliver man

sent darts and fierce battles against the baby, the young and the adult Jesus, trying every means to bring Him down from fulfilling and winning the battle of man's deliverance. In all this, Jesus didn't shift His gaze from the essence of His coming, and He kept pushing through till he took up the cross and was led up to Golgotha to die for the sins of the whole world, hence paying the debts of sin for all men; even for those that didn't believe in Him yet. To the glory of God, the battle could have been lost if the prince of this world had come and found a hold on Jesus (John 14:30). Jesus showed man the way of the cross by being a champion in it. This act of Jesus carries the potentiality of delivering any man from the rule of sin, for as many as can come to Him, believe in Him and confess with their mouth His Lordship.

Salvation from Death:

After the fall of man, death began to reign over man. At a point in time, God was so displeased with the way man continued to live his life that he decreed a reduction in the time man can spend here on earth (Gen 6:3) and that His spirit would not contend with h anymore. The state is a terrible one for man, as his days on earth is characterized by the fear of death (Heb 2:15).

"Nevertheless, death reigned from the time of Adam to the time of Moses, even over those who did not sin by breaking a command, as did Adam, who is a pattern of one to come; For if, by the trespass of one man, death reigned through that one man…"- Rom 5:14 & 17a. This is a serious problem for man, but thanks to Jesus, who championed the deliverance of man from death and its attending fear. Jesus came in the likeness of man to win the battle over death and gave life to as many that come to Him.

"...I have come that they may have life and to have it to the full"- John 10:10

Rom 5:18 further showed the results of Jesus' sacrifice,

"Consequently, just as one trespass resulted in the condemnation for all people, so also one righteous act resulted in justification and life for all people."

The fear of death is done away with among those that come to Christ; they live life to the fullest.

Salvation from Satan's dominion:

Since man fell, the Lordship and rulership of the earth were handed over to the Devil as against God's plan. Jesus came leading all the way to fight for the deliverance of the earth from the dominion of Satan and handed over the authority on earth and in heaven to the ones who dearly follows him with full assurance of faith. The scripture says

"Since the children have flesh and blood, He too shared in their humanity so that by His death He might break the power of Him who holds the power of death- that is, the devil"- Heb 2:14.

Jesus championed many things for us: our new nature in God and the destruction of the dividing wall between God and us, reconciling us back to Him (Eph 2:14). No man has ever done this and can ever do it. Jesus also, by His blood and flesh, opened a new and living way into the heart of the Father, the Holies of Holies (Heb 10:19-20). Jesus wrought great things for every man on earth and was finally able to put the Devil where he should be, under our feet. Jesus became the only man to excel in all spheres of life without mincing words.

The most unprecedented of all is the promise of a new life with neither pain nor death. But for these things to come to us, many had labored. Many faithful men and women have made sacrifices to have us in the kingdom. Jesus made us know that we will enjoy life eternal. He brought about our reunion with the Father again. He thought us peace, love, and unity (Proverbs 20:28).

Abraham gave us faith. He thought the people that without faith, it is hard to please God. Enoch was a man of faith too. He was a champion. He walked with God believing in his promises, and he was spared from death. Deborah was a champion; she led Barak to defeat Sisera and Jabin. Moses was a champion; he led one of the most significant survival expeditions by taking the entire Israelites out of Egypt. He was an able leader who was never afraid but steadfast in his course. The missionaries that followed the apostles ensured that the faith they were given did not slip off their hands. Martin Luther, John Calvin, Zig Ziglar, Tyndale, and the rest followed. These champions ensured that there was a quick spread of Christianity. They championed the opportunity for individuals to have the Bible in their hands. Everyone can now read with minimal guidance and understand, unlike before. Therefore these set of people that laid the path for others to follow were champions.

They could be burned at the stake. Their books or the Bible they were distributing could be considered among the heretical books not fit for reading as the authorities would have decided. They saw punishment staring them in the face, but they refused to be intimidated. They remained focused and determined. Therefore, you must know that whatever we have that is looking very good now and interesting had at a point before been very challenging; only that people of courage never relented. Missionaries sailed so many seas and rivers to give us the Good News. Had they been afraid and not ready to stand firm, there would have been difficulty in reaching the goal of proclaiming the gospel to all nations. The missionaries went to different places and different lands meeting diverse cultures, some very difficult to penetrate and others not so difficult, but challenging in terms of exposure to environmental hazards. These unrelenting champions brought us to the realization of the salvation of Christ.

In the beginning, we examined who a champion is, and in closing, I introduced you to the greatest champion of all times, that is our Lord and Savior Jesus Christ. My point here is you are a champion. Yes, you heard me. You are a Champion! No matter what the Devil is telling you, or making you feel or go through. Remember that others have gone through worst and you are not the first and will certainly not be the last. Man, get up, and have faith, cast all your burdens on Jesus and leave it there; focus on your plans and desires. Follow the map I have carefully prepared for you in this book, and you will see that the light in you will shine brighter every day until it begins to give light to others. This knowledge is the source of faith you need to keep your head above the waters so you can attempt great things for the sake of Christ.

Furthermore, Joel Osteen has this to say to you, "Even though dirt may get thrown on your dream, instead of letting it get buried, the true mark of a champion is to keep shaking it off. Look for new ways to move forward. Believe for new opportunities." Trust me, Jesus knows you, and he knows you can be a champion because he has already opened the way for you. You need to know that lying silently within you is the capacity to bring to life a wonder on earth, you can't afford to settle for less dear reader, you need to arise and find that light and keep your focus on it, you are set for great things on this earth and the Bible says this to you

"For the creation waits in eager expectation for the children of God to be revealed"- Rom 8:19.

Arise, dear beloved, as a spiritual champion. I wish you Good luck in your journey.

REFERENCES

African Leadership Magazine (2017) 7 Reasons why Nelson Mandela was a great leader. Retrieved from http://africanleadership.co.uk/7-reasons-nelson-mandela-great-leader/

Anirudh (2017). 10 Major accomplishment of Nelson Mandela. Retrieved from https://learnodo-newtonic.com/nelson-mandela-accomplishments

Features V (2015). Top 5 Martin Luther King Jr. Achievements. Retrieved from http://www.videtteonline.com/features/top-martin-luther-king-jr-achievements/article_2f242ca3-0e63-5da4-b6ed-ba62c50a12ab.html

Historyplex (2018). Interesting facts about Abraham Lincoln. Retrieved from https://historyplex.com/interesting-facts-about-abraham-lincoln

Holy Bible NIV, KJV and NKJV

Biblical Nuggets for my daily victories- Rev Dr. Gabriel Oluwasegun

Mount Vernon (n,d). Key Facts about George Washington. Retrieved from https://www.mountvernon.org/george-washington/key-facts/

www.ingramcontent.com/pod-product-compliance
Lightning Source LLC
Chambersburg PA
CBHW070758020526
44118CB00036B/1936